Why am I Afraid to be Assertive?

PATRICIA MANSFIELD brings together people
from both the public sector and the private sector
who are expected to reach the highest levels in
their respective organisations. The book's emphasis is
on change, understanding it and teaching it.

Why am I Afraid to be Assertive?

Patricia Mansfield

Series Editor
Phillip Hodson

Fount
An Imprint of HarperCollins*Publishers*

Fount Paperbacks is an Imprint of
HarperCollins*Religious*
Part of HarperCollins*Publishers*
77–85 Fulham Palace Road, London W6 8JB

First published in Great Britain
in 1994 by Fount Paperbacks

1   3   5   7   9   10   8   6   4   2

Text copyright © 1994 Patricia Mansfield
Preface copyright © 1994 Phillip Hodson

Patricia Mansfield asserts the moral right to
be identified as the author of this work

A catalogue record for this book is
available from the British Library

ISBN 0 00 627671-7

Printed and bound in Great Britain by
HarperCollinsManufacturing Glasgow

Contents

Acknowledgements

I want to thank a number of people for the help and support they have given me. Dave, my mentor, who listened and listened and listened to the outpourings of my soul and did lots of research for me. To Ricky and Sue for their support, love and hard work. To Bridget for her practical help, and finally to my children, Robert and Catherine, for always being there, loving, supporting and keeping my feet on the ground.

Preface

One of the great difficulties in life is that if you can't ask for what you want you have to put up with what you get. The blight of what's called low self-esteem lies at the heart of this problem and tends to undermine most attempts at personal happiness.

This is all the more true in a British setting where the historic emphasis has been on stiffening the upper lip, turning the other cheek, promoting 'service before self' or deferring to elders who 'know better'. Such qualities may have their place but no longer work as a total creed. They've done nothing to help the less resilient or under-confident members of society, let alone the poor, the weak or those without privilege. People with low self-esteem simply become silent victims of the social system.

We also know that faulty self-image and esteem inevitably result when children grow up in very unhappy or insecure circumstances. So regardless of society's values, if young people are abused or rejected they become adults who don't really know how to ask for what they want. Most will be mute; others, by contrast, will shout long and loud for everything they've been denied in an equally inappropriate fashion. Both sets, as well as those who've been conditiond into passivity, need to learn how to act with more self-assertion.

This, of course, does not mean more aggressively. For example, I am not acting ASSERTIVELY when I threaten to kill a pedestrian who bumps into me. I am only exercising my neurotic insecurities and will feel just as insecure the next time someone clumsily crosses my path. In order to assert my ENTIRE self, I need to remain in command both of my emotions and the encounter.

I think the real usefulness of Patricia Mansfield's book lies in her ability to make this distinction PERSONALLY clear. She's been there, she's grown up with a number of family difficulties, she's seen the problem from the inside as well as the outside, and she's tested all the suggested solutions. If you've ever been through the mill, this book is for you – it is impossible not to identify the problem from the varied and almost un-connected references Patricia assembles. One person who read the manuscript said it's like a 'Bible' on assertion – from Genesis to Revelation.

Be that as it may, this book is comprehensive and explains exactly how you may grow up feeling disabled by negative remarks and treatment, yet take steps to correct the picture and enjoy work, play and relationships in a more contented future.

Phillip Hodson

Introduction

As you work your way through this book, it will lead you along the path to assertiveness. It will help you think about the steps you can take to do something positive to improve your self-esteem. You will learn to think about loving yourself more, about improving your confidence and finding out what's holding you back. You will get to know your inner self better. Knowing yourself and understanding why you do what you do will give a stronger foundation to your life and enable you to get ahead. The book is also about my own search to find answers about how the mind works and why we behave as we do, and most importantly how to stop doing things that are spoiling our lives. It gives a little taste of realistic changes you can make. It shows how an inner strength can make you more responsible for what happens in your future, no matter what happened in the past.

I think you will find this book easy to read. I hope to make the road to assertiveness easy and full of delight.

Assertiveness improved my life. Working in a boarding school where parents paid huge fees to ensure their offspring's education, and seeing first-hand the difference education and wealth makes to a person's confidence and self-assuredness, even in small boys, was quite an eye-opener for me. I'd had little of either.

I realized at once how much I needed to grow in order to match these assertive little people in my care. During my time as school matron I did a vast amount of reading on ways to improve the quality of life. This sowed the seeds for my first tentative steps towards the new asssertive person I hoped to become. It was not until I finally decided to give up my job there that I made a positive decision to do something constructive about my shyness and lack of self-esteem.

When I left, one of the boys stood up to give a little speech of thanks to me. Then followed some precious moments when many of the boys gave me presents and flowers. I was overwhelmed with feelings of sadness but of pride too. How badly I wanted to stand up and say a few words of thanks in return! But some kind of inner demon seemed to have me by the throat. I felt fear rise up within me. My legs turned to jelly and I was so consumed with panic that I could not even stand up. Frozen to my seat I mumbled a shy 'Thank you'. It was not until one of my little charges rushed up and gave me a hug that the spell was broken and I was able to relax a little.

I have had experience as a State Registered Nurse, Matron at a boarding school, and as a bereavement counsellor. I have been involved in personal development for the last eight years. I have trained in counselling, Hypnotherapy and mental health. I have worked on hospital radio and I'm a qualified marriage therapist. I have also worked as a co-ordinator for SANELINE, a mental health charity, and have been involved with the training of the volunteers for their helpline. And as a counsellor with Family Matters, a charity who help survivors of child abuse and their families.

My main occupation has, however, been writing. I began with a medical, and later an agony, column in the *Northern Echo* in Darlington, and then moved on to the *London Evening News* in Fleet Street, the *Daily Star* and *Take A Break* magazine, the largest selling women's magazine in Britain.

Along the way, I have learned how to make clearer, more

specific requests. Before, I used to waffle on about what I wanted, hoping someone would give it to me and then when they didn't, feeling sorry for myself. I learnt how to say no in ways which were firm and yet inoffensive and to accept other people's noes without feeling hurt or rejected myself. I found out about body language and how it can help you to get your point across. Perhaps most important of all, I now know how to recognize and manage my anger. I discovered how easy it can be to give and, more importantly for a non-assertive person, to accept, compliments. This had been very difficult for me in the past. I began to take the initiative.

None of this happened overnight and I still have a long way to go. But now I feel like an evangelist spreading the word on assertiveness. Learn to like yourself more, find a confidence you never knew existed and the world will become a newer, happier, and more fulfilling place.

What Being Assertive Means

Being assertive is all about believing in yourself but respecting the feelings and needs of others too. It means finding new ways to express yourself while recognizing your own strengths and weaknesses. It is to behave in a way which enables you to act in your own best interests, to stand up for yourself without becoming unduly anxious, to affirm your own feelings honestly and comfortably – even if they are different from the opinions of others – and to exercise your own rights without denying the rights of other people.

In order to be assertive it is vital not to be worried or preoccupied that your behaviour doesn't fit in with other people's images and ideas of how you 'ought' to be. That is their problem – not yours.

You are able to express your thoughts clearly and openly. You can achieve the kind of relationship, friendships and life style you want. You will find a way to handle awkward situations in a way that neither upsets nor offends. You will be aware of what you are saying or doing. You will listen to and question your own thoughts and actions. You will become pro-active: that is, you will make things happen rather than just sitting back and allowing things to happen to you.

Most people don't face up to their own wants and needs. They have great difficulty in asserting them and thus they feel confused and unsure of themselves when others try to assert theirs. When others assert themselves their own feelings seem to be annihilated and the confusion and uncertainty becomes magnified out of all proportion.

From childhood we spend a lot of time consciously and subconsciously acquiring skills that will help us in our day-to-day life. These learned actions and reactions affect others and are the building blocks of our personality. You learn that the intonation of a voice can subtly modify the meaning of words. You learn how to use a smile. You learn how vital first impressions can be. In fact you have a higher level of assertiveness skills than you may realize. Even so, if you feel you do not create the impression you want, you need a few skills to help you on your way. You must change your programming and the conditioning of your childhood.

Success in personal, social and business life depends very much on what people think of us. Some people seem to have a gift for relating well to others and giving a 'good' impression.

Non-assertive people, on the other hand, mull over events that have happened. They waste time dwelling on what they MIGHT have said long after the opportunity to be assertive has passed.

A non-assertive person often responds too vigorously to a situation he or she finds difficult. All too frequently non-assertive people have been brought up in an authoritarian home. When children are brought up to have all their decisions made for them they feel that their own views are valueless unless approved by their parents. Alternatively, a child brought up in a far too passive environment where every one of his opinions is treated as sacrosanct may grow up to believe that the opinions of others are not valid. In an environment where everyone has the right to think, want and feel anything they like, life becomes less of a battleground. Compromises can be found at every level and life becomes sweeter.

In a non-assertive relationship people are rarely clear about what they want – even to themselves. A non-assertive person may invent a set of 'I shoulds' based on messages they've picked up during their life. Then they expect others (who have received other messages) to conform to theirs. They make these others feel undermined, ignorant and guilty for having different opinions.

It is important to remember that in an honest and assertive world you will not always get your own way – nor will everyone see the world through your eyes. People won't always agree with you or necessarily like you. But real relationships and friendships are not dependent on the fact that each likes or agrees with the other on everything they believe or do.

Assertiveness has frequently been linked to aggression which is interpreted as a 'masculine characteristic'. As a result, in an effort not to appear masculine, women avoided behaviour they considered unattractive and unfeminine. Fortunately nowadays things are changing and it is not only men who are beginning to gain the confidence to express themselves in an honest and straightforward way. Women are emerging from the straitjacket of the Victorian era.

If you can relate to any of these feelings then I'm sure you have already felt motivated to change. Becoming assertive is a big step towards freeing yourself from self-denying behaviour.

YOUR JOURNAL

Get yourself a journal in which to record your progress. Keep a daily record of the new goals you are going to set yourself. Record the feelings that arise when you try something new for the first time and how you feel when you achieve it. Note your successes and your failures but each time something doesn't quite turn out as you wish, remind yourself that each mistake is a step towards your goal. It is something from which you can learn and which you can try to avoid in future. If you do the same thing again – so what? No one gets everything right the first or even the second time.

Draw pictures in your journal, list the non-assertive traits you think apply to you and say where you think they came from.

Write about your dreams. Get to know yourself and what made you the person you are today. Be honest with yourself. This journal is for your eyes and your eyes alone. It is a positive and personal reappraisal.

Some people will say they cannot write and be so intimidated by the prospect of keeping a journal that they put it off. This fear probably goes back to school days where everything they wrote was judged. You need not show your private diary to a soul. No one is going to analyse it or criticize it. You are writing about how things have been for you in the past, how you coped and how you plan to cope better in the future. By identifying what has gone wrong in your life and by facing and working through the dilemmas and the false beliefs about yourself, you can cast off redundant baggage. Don't worry about being self-conscious.

As you work towards the emergence of the real you, the more you write, the more powerfully will the images stay in your mind. Give yourself half an hour each day at a convenient time. (If your day is crammed then spend half an hour when you go to bed at night.) Go over the past day and plan the next goal – whether it be smiling at a stranger, saying no to someone for the first time, or accepting a compliment graciously. It is true that we learn largely from the things we do but we can learn from our thoughts and our dreams in much the same way. Reflect upon your own night-time dreams and create your own daydreams. Dreaming, thinking and planning allow you to try out new behaviour in advance. When you need it you will already have it rehearsed and perfected in your own mind. Even then you won't get it right straight away so – practise, practise, practise! I will discuss dream-work further in chapter 11.

NON-ASSERTIVE BEHAVIOUR TYPES

There are three main types of non-assertive behaviour:

Avoidance Behaviour

Avoidance behaviour shows itself by fear of the reaction of others. It evades honest confrontation. Those who use avoidance behaviour agree with everything and everyone and have few original opinions or ideas of their own. They ignore any infringement of their own rights. They are generally indecisive, submissive and avoid disagreements of any kind. They are manipulated by others, and often go along with the majority or a powerful group when really they don't agree with them. If attacked they make excuses and keep lots of feelings of injustice buried inside.

Aggressive Behaviour

Aggressive behaviour is often the result of an accumulation of anger. When we feel ignored, cheated or put upon we can feel childishly angry or hurt and may be tempted to have a tantrum or burst out with angry words out of proportion to the situation. Others become wary of these situations. They may keep silent to avoid an outburst leading you to feel you are being assertive and in control when in fact the opposite is true.

It is often more difficult for the aggressive person to acknowledge the need for help since he or she is accustomed to feeling in control of his environment. A relationship based on the aggression of one person is unhealthy and usually worsens unless the aggressive person actively pursues change. If you think this may apply to you ask yourself these questions:

- Do others seldom engage with you in discussion?
- Do you usually feel you win arguments?
- Do you feel you 'rule' your home and your workplace?

If the answer to these questions is yes, then it is quite likely that you alienate those around you and you will find them either trying to 'get back' at you at some point in the future, or simply cutting off from you. Do you think that alienation of those close to you is a worthwhile price to pay for being top dog? Assertiveness may often have the same result but with fewer lost relationships en route.

Sadly, this aggressive anger is often directed towards someone who has done very little harm. Frequently it is the partner or an innocent child who bears the brunt of the anger, and used as the scapegoat. The fury released during these moments of immoderation and the result of that build-up of frustration, self-doubt and feelings of low self-worth, is like a demon. Your frustration must lessen so your anger and your excessive aggression will fade, until serenity prevails.

Aggressive people who are full of bravado and arrogance appear to have a good sense of self-worth but in truth they are desperately trying to hide from others (and incidentally from themselves) their true feelings. Inside they feel just as bad as the quiet mouse who sits in the corner afraid to open his mouth to venture an opinion.

Accommodating Behaviour

Accommodating behaviour is frequently misinterpreted. It can lead to others taking advantage of you. I am sure you have heard people say, 'If you make a doormat of yourself then people are bound to walk all over you'. This is exactly what non-assertive people do. Accommodating behaviour is used to evade friction of any kind. It leaves others uncertain of your feelings and therefore often they are disregarded or you are totally ignored. People who use this type of behaviour often find themselves 'lumbered' with tasks they did not really want to do. Managers find it very difficult to refuse or be firm with their employees or colleagues and therefore nigh on impossible to correct them when they are wrong. These are clear examples of non-assertion. Avoidance of conflict is the main objective of accommodating behaviour.

The older we get the more difficult it is to change – but it is never too late. The difficulty is that making changes takes courage. Often it seems simpler and more comfortable to fall back into old ways – even if they do shackle us and hold us back.

Reacting assertively means being totally honest. For instance when you don't undertand something, someone may imply that you are stupid or unintelligent. It is nonsense to imagine we should have complete understanding of everything. The chances are that there are also others who don't understand. So if you don't understand something it is assertive to say so. Someone will always be pleased to air their 'superior' knowledge. The others who have not understood will be relieved to have another explanation – and say so, once you have broken the ice.

Being honest also means not pretending to care about things you feel you 'ought' to care about. Pretence doesn't help anyone. Sincerity is always recognizable for what it is. If you are to run your life in the way you want, you are the one to decide what *you* care about.

The inference is that if you do not voice approval of everything that others do they won't like you any more. But this is school playground behaviour. Adults cannot all approve of the same things. We do not all have the same wants or needs. We cannot possibly agree with everyone in this world. Co-operation and compromise are never dependent on agreeing with everything and everyone.

An assertive person does not have to justify his or her reasons for doing or not doing something. By justifying yourself you are implying that what you are doing or saying is not good enough. Remember too that you are allowed to make mistakes. It gives others a false sense of confidence if they can make you feel valueless because you have made a mistake. An assertive person doesn't allow this to happen. As I have said, there is no such thing as a fault-free existence.

An assertive person does not have to make him or herself responsible for solving the problems of the world. People may try to manipulate you by asking you to do a favour. Let us say they ask you to pick up their son from school. This means you will miss an important meeting, so you say it is difficult for you. Your manipulator says, 'But that means little Jimmy will be sitting on the school steps until I finish work.' An unassertive person will at this point become loaded with guilt and take responsibility for this person's child. But it is not your problem nor is it your responsibility.

An assertive person may have a different opinion on a given

topic from the one he had last week. A manipulative person may try to make him feel guilty by reminding him that this contradicts something he has said previously. In the light of better judgement you and everyone else have a perfect right to change your mind, to be flexible or even inconsistent. There is no law that says that what you said before should be cast in stone for eternity.

YOU HAVE THE RIGHT TO BE ASSERTIVE

Many 'RIGHTS' have been laid down by different psychologists over the years. Here is a sample of those rights. I am sure you can think up a few more of your own once you get the idea. Write them down in your journal and read them through whenever you are at odds with yourself about how you should handle a problem.

These are your rights:

- You have the right to ask for what you want (and accept that the other person has the right to refuse).
- You have the right to say 'I don't care'.
- You have the right to be illogical and not to have to justify yourself.
- You have the right to make your own decisions and cope with the consequences.
- You have the right to choose whether or not you should be responsible for solving other people's problems.
- You have the right not to know about something, or not to understand.
- You have the right to make mistakes.
- You have the right to be successful.
- You have the right to change your mind.
- You have the right to privacy.
- You have the right to be alone and independent.
- You have the right to make changes and become more assertive.
- You have the right to say yes or no for yourself.
- You have the right to express your own opinions.

Once you accept that you have these rights then it should follow that you will accept that others, too, have these rights.

CHAPTER 2

What Lies Behind The Fears That Hold You Back?

Have you any idea of what it is that lies behind the fears that stop you from getting on with your life? An internal struggle is going on between the extremes of self-love and self-loathing in most of us. It is as true of the rich and famous as it is of the poor and unknown; it is as true of extroverts as it is of introverts and it is as true of everyone you imagine is brimming with self-confidence as it is of the nervous and self-effacing people that we all know. It is true of me and I'm pretty sure it is true of you.

All the experiences – the criticisms, the put-downs, the negative and positive statements we've been subjected to over the years have helped to make us what we are today. We are told when our behaviour is 'good' and we are rewarded with loving looks and supportive actions. Later on, behaviour we learned when we were small becomes modified by our peers and teachers at school, but personality growth is constant and I can't say often enough that it is never too late to learn new skills.

Normal family life leaves all kinds of records playing in our minds which can haunt us for the rest of our lives. 'Children should be seen and not heard', they 'must speak when they are spoken to' and they 'must do as their parents say and not as they do'. We are told to 'turn the other cheek', and are reminded that 'the meek shall inherit the earth'. And how many times were you told to 'know your place'? The British class system is less repressive nowadays but it is still true that money, privilege and education bring with them a certain amount of self-assuredness and assertiveness. Most of us do not have this kind of background and consequently we behave in a more repressed and restrained way, conditioned by our upbringing.

Restrained, well-behaved children who quietly conform and who do not question are rewarded and those that 'make waves' are brought down, punished or humiliated. Children are reprimanded for being strong-willed, and having ideas of their own. Even a small baby in the cradle who is quiet and who doesn't protest is rewarded with smiles, strokes and soft encouraging voices. It is generally accepted by doctors and psychiatrists and those that deal with childcare that many of our personality traits are developed during those early months. Our personalities go on to be moulded by such factors as our position in the family, our sex and as many of us are painfully aware, by favouritism displayed by parents or older brothers or sisters.

In our schools, well-meaning teachers may experience a variety of different responses from youngsters in their efforts to treat all children equally. A simple remark like 'please get on with your work' directed to a child who is peeping at a comic under the desk can evoke different responses from different children. One child may think the teacher is unfair. He may sulk or shed a few tears. Another may think he's been 'picked on' because he knows his friend is also reading and has not been discovered. He is likely to defend himself and kick his friend under the table. Another may blush, feel guilty, say sorry, and promise not to do it again. Yet another, more wily, child, may explain that the comic is of 'educational value'. And I'm sure we all know of someone who would have broken down into floods of tears because the teacher raised his voice. The list of reactions is endless. Programmed by the conditioning of early childhood we may all develop our own set of reactions in given situations.

In the past, school teachers have, without any malicious intent, continued to squash children's spontaneity by rewarding the non-assertive child and punishing those who show initiative or curiosity or who buck the system. It was only recently that physical punishment, in school, like the slipper and the cane, were made illegal. Unfortunately much of the emotional damage it did is still around in society. However, more and more people are discovering that you can 'knock the devil in but it's more difficult to knock him out again'.

Even the children who have been lucky enough to have their assertive behaviour admired and praised at home sometimes found it was condemned once they entered the classroom – not only by teachers but by their peers. Spontaneity in learning is so often conditioned out of us by the time we are ready to start out in life as independent people. And many people rear children of their own in the same rigid way before realizing the dangers. Thus our social structures are perpetuated.

By the time young people are ready to go out into the world their behaviour patterns are often already badly impaired. Once these non-assertive youngsters start work they feel obliged to go along with everything their employers say. They are often scared to speak up for themselves even if they know they have been wronged, they are too lacking in self-esteem to express ideas of their own and they are terrified of asking for anything for themselves. If they manage to find a job and keep it for any length of time then eventually they must think about asking for a rise. Putting a request in for an increase in salary is a particularly difficult thing to do for non-assertive people because they fear rejection. They hold back. They don't get that pay rise and so their sense of self-worth sinks even further.

Young people starting out in life who find that new experiences do not conform to what they have learned as accepted behaviour are apt to panic. They watch others closely and try to adapt in order to meet with approval. They change their way of dressing, speaking and their behaviour to fit in with their new environment. Again, different people react in different ways. Some find that the exaggeration of any behaviour that does not meet with approval gets a powerful response.

17

This type of behaviour can give them a lift. They may feel as if they are actually standing up for themselves or making a point, but often the behaviour goes on to become antisocial. Some skinheads or hell's angels who dress in unconventional ways, who snub their noses at convention and who display bizarre behaviour and speak in outlandish ways are clear examples. Others avoid situations where they fear conflict or disapproval. This opting out is not very successful either. It is digging themselves a deeper pit of un-assertiveness and to climb out of it becomes increasingly difficult.

Some non-assertive people find that the answer is to tell lies. They are scared to express themselves honestly because they have such low self-esteem. They feel people will disapprove of them or put them down if they are honest. These people have limited success in the short term because strangers may believe what they say and be impressed. Their egos are massaged for a few precious moments but once others who may get to know them better see through their behaviour they lose respect and find it hard to retain friendship. Thus they lose out on two levels.

Gender also teaches different lessons. Women, for example, are still generally expected to do more around the house than men. This stereotyping too is changing but still parents unconsciously replay the records from their childhood that they hear in their heads. These records tell them that it's 'not manly' for boys to do housework. They tend to let boys get away with much more. Records like 'Boys will be boys' and 'Young ladies don't do things like that', 'That is woman's/man's work' are heard regularly. Without realizing it, we have been programmed to behave in certain ways. The result is that many women and some men are too passive. They allow others (usually their partners) to demean them. They make it easy for their partners to treat them as second-class citizens. Too many men believe it is perfectly okay to treat their partners in this way. To be described as 'under a woman's thumb' is just about the worst insult a man can suffer. And all because they are caught offering to do a bit of washing up!

Assertive behaviour helps people to deal with each other

equally – to 'do as we would be done by', as the old adage so rightly says.

THE FAMILY

Different families bring out different behaviour patterns in their members. Family situations and their sometimes complicated relationships have a huge influence on the future behaviour of the children in them:-

In a large family with four or more children, the situation is likely to be unique, but one child – usually the girl – from sheer necessity, often takes on the role of stand-in mum. It is different for other members of the family. Boys and younger girls are frequently given more freedom. One young woman, 'Lynda', said that she had fallen into the 'stand-in mum' role as young as eight years old! Her mother had five babies after her. She had one older brother but neither he nor the younger siblings helped around the house, except in a token way. She did what she felt she had to do automatically, but now after getting involved in a relationship where she was treated as a virtual slave, she realized she had to make some changes if she was to get any respect at all. It was clear that the encouraging praise from both parents and other members of the family had made her feel really important in her housewifely role, but later she started to resent the way she was treated. So many problems surfaced when she tried to break free that she stopped trying and settled down to being a pleaser and a doormat. It was less trouble.

When she finally plucked up the courage to break away from her family she set up home with someone who was like her father in many ways. She settled easily into the 'pleasing' role. It was second nature. Only later when she talked to other women about their relationships did she begin to see that she was not handling things very well. I met her when she was just beginning to climb out of the non-assertive pit she'd helped dig for herself and was making some demands on her own behalf.

Children who have one sibling of the opposite sex, and who grow up in a more traditional family, soon pick up the clear-cut gender differences. Girls see their mother sewing, cooking and doing household tasks day after day. They become aware that she is fulfilling the caring, supporting and nurturing role and notice that her priority is always to please Dad. The boy sees his dad being treated in a special manner. He learns to expect that sort of treatment for himself. He learns that Dad is the disciplinarian in the family and that Mum is softer, more malleable. He sees his father working out the finances and paying the bills and he grows up expecting to be in control of these things too. Of course each family is different but it's easy to see how easily these natural behaviour patterns slip into our subconscious without our having to try.

In David's home, Father was treated like a tin god. As soon as his car drew up in the drive Mum began scurrying round making final adjustments to the table; she'd quickly tidy her hair and put on some lipstick. The children's faces would be wiped clean and then, as if by magic, as soon as Dad's coat was off, his dinner would appear steaming on the table. This was what Dad expected and David grew up expecting it too. His first wife was not prepared to treat him with such 'respect' – nor was his second. It wasn't until he sought counselling and began to accept men and women as equals that he even went a little way towards changing his attitude.

'Jane' grew up in a similar household. She hated the way her mum used to grovel to her dad and agreed with everything he said. She hated the way her mother never voiced her own opinions or stood up for herself. She swore she would be different, but when after six years of marriage she found herself constantly giving in to her husband's wishes – particularly his desire to have her stay at home when really she wanted to work and see more of life; when she found herself dieting for the umpteenth time because he'd mentioned he could 'pinch more than an inch'; when she found herself watching the clock when he was due home so everything would be 'perfect' when he walked in, and worst of all, when she found herself agreeing to sex when she really was not in the mood – she decided enough was enough. She'd lost her identity and her confidence. Jane seemed to have been swallowed up in their union somewhere. She'd become Mrs Brown. She'd lost her individuality. In spite of all her ideals and her loathing of the way her mother behaved, that programming, those messages inside her head, had worked their way through from her psyche to actuality and she was acting them out. Once she realized what had happened she signed up for an assertiveness class to support her while she tried to make the changes necessary for her to regain her identity and ultimately, in so doing, her self-respect.

In families where there are rigid rules of behaviour, different messages come through. These children grow up with a completely different set of messages. Messages can give a person a clear shape to their world and instil the confidence that comes from knowing just where you're at, but at the same time they can damage a person's self-esteem by consuming their vitality, leaving no room for originality.

Fathers may behave like institution-trained disciplinarians, listing and judging household chores that the children are expected to do. Mothers may refuse to let their children watch television programmes, and vet their friends and their activities. Parents who set ridiculous unbending bedtime rules and expect perfect table and conversational manners are all affecting the child's personality in some way. Children from families such as these are apt to grow up continually trying to come up to everyone else's standards, bewildering not only themselves, but also those around them. Boys in this type of household tend to be treated more harshly. They often live in terror of what Dad will do if they misbehave (and frequently Dad fulfils his threats to punish in a variety of ways). However, eventually, they do seem to ultimately manage to gain more freedom than the girls who do not receive such stringent treatment. The girls grow up expecting their actions to be monitored. They are aware of every gesture, how they sit, how they walk, how they stand. They follow Mum's submissive behaviour and are constantly seeking approval. They learn to pout and do the 'sweet little girl' routine and for the most part it seems to work.

'Jean' and 'Robin' had domineering but kind parents. When Jean was four and her brother just five, a family holiday was planned. Mother, in true regimental form, had laid out the children's holiday clothes, books and swimwear on their respective beds and left their small suitcases ready so these 'grown-up' little people could do their own packing. Robin was the first to close his case. Puffing and panting he dragged his little blue suitcase to the top of the stairs. He asked his dad to help him carry it down but Dad said, 'Come on – you are a man now – not a wimp. Carry it down yourself.' And a tearful Robin half dragged and half carried the tiny suitcase down the stairs.

A few moments later Jean appeared at the top of the stairs and with her best coquettish look she said, 'I need a big strong man to help me'. Her dad looked at Mum, smiled and said, 'How can I resist?' He swept upstairs and carried both her and her case down.

Robin grew up to never ask for help. He refused even to ask the way if he was lost. He HAD to find the way on his own or he felt he'd lost face. It became automatic for Jean to put on the sweet little girl routine. The pattern repeated itself in her relationships. She found it helped her to get her own way. But this routine never works for long. After several failed relationships she had to ask herself if she shouldn't be taking some responsiblity for herself. She worked hard on more assertive methods of getting what she wanted and gradually created more balanced and healthy relationships.

Messages from our various religious backgrounds, picked up unconsciously as we develop, indicate that such qualities as humility, self-denial and self-sacrifice are not compatible with feelings of self-worth, confidence and the ability to stand up for ourselves.

The institutions of our society have taught us to feel bad about defending our rights, about feeling good without feeling guilty. They underpin deep-seated fears about expressing opinions which may be different, inventive or controversial. This programming has limited the creativity of many intelligent and capable people. It has held them back at work and in social situations. Most importantly it has put huge obstacles in the way of forming healthy, loving, personal relationships.

The memories, buried in our subconscious, of embarrassment or hurt when simple childhood requests have been turned down stops us from making requests today. We are scared that any of our requests be refused and we magnify the accompanying feelings which arise. But we don't only limit these magnified feelings to our own inner thoughts. We transfer them to others too. We might also become apprehensive that our request may embarrass someone else who may not want to do what we would like them to do.

We also hold back because of ingrained messages we have received about good manners. We are frequently terrified that we may offend someone by asking for something for ourselves. How many times have you heard people say, 'oh I couldn't ask him this or that!'; 'he'd be furious, he'd be upset, he'd be angry, or offended'; or 'she'd go mad!'; 'she'll hit the roof!'; 'she'd have my guts for garters' . . . Ask yourself honestly – how on earth do we know how someone else will react? The answer is purely and simply that WE DO NOT. We guess. We try to read people's minds and OFTEN we are wrong. Unless we actually ask and wait for the response there is no way of knowing. Therefore, we must ask and then learn how to cope with the responses instead of just being negative. Remember always think positively.

There are a hundred and one factors which influence the way we develop. The way your parents or close family members have previously treated you has a huge influence. Were you loved for being you or did they want you to be different? Did they criticize you constantly, never praising you, or did they praise you more than criticize? Were you praised so much that you were embarrassed? Or in such a way that you consider yourself to be invincible? Were you constantly compared with someone else or many others? Did your parents practise what they preached? Or did they do one thing and expect you to do another? Were they happy or unhappy? Did they have a positive or negative outlook on life? Was the relationship balanced? Were they good communicators? How did they relate to others? Did they put on a front for the world and show a different side in the home or were they always consistent?

Was your life style sheltered or were you constantly thrust into the limelight? Were you forced to socialize or compete? Did you travel much or have a great deal of change in your life? Were you brought up in a religious household? If you were, did your religion make you feel good about yourself or believe yourself a sinner? Were your religious teachers optimistic or pessimistic? Were men given more responsibilities than women? What was your position in the family? Were you an only child? The eldest, the youngest or in the middle? Were you given responsibility for looking after younger children? How did you get on with your brothers and sisters? Did you look up to the older ones or fear them? Were they more or less successful than you?

How did you cope at school? Were you a pet or a pest? Were you picked on or punished? Were you bullied, left out or welcomed by other children? Were you successful or did you feel a failure? Were you from a privileged or underprivileged background? Did you have all you needed for a comfortable life or did you have to go without? Were you physically, sexually or emotionally abused? Did any close members of your family die or leave the family home?

There are a hundred and one different scenarios that could be considered here, but I am sure you can think of things in your childhood that may have contributed to the non-assertive behaviour you display today. Once you understand yourself better and can hear more clearly the records and the messages that are playing in your head, the legacies of your upbringing that are spoiling things for you now, then the sooner you can begin to make changes, and start to take charge of your life. You will free yourself to make assertive decisions without the constant need to please and you will discover ways to put your relationships on a more even keel.

STUMBLING BLOCKS

A universal stumbling block on the assertiveness ladder is the idea, widely believed in our society, that it is not acceptable to talk about our own accomplishments. We receive a barrage of messages telling us that it is 'sinful' to be vain or conceited.

For too long we have had false modesty drummed into us with phrases like 'self-praise is no recommendation'. But if you don't love yourself in the first place, how on earth can you expect anyone else to care for you? And if you don't love yourself how can you go on to love anyone else? Loving and looking after yourself means taking pride in yourself and having self-respect. To have pride in oneself and self-respect doesn't mean you have to be selfish or to ignore the needs of others.

Most people feel embarrassed about admitting their strengths, so they pretend they cannot cope even when they can. Soon they begin to believe their deception themselves. It is considered 'bad form' to 'sing our own praises'. We have been programmed to find realistic, confident people from different cultures who are aware of their own abilities, unpalatable. They find us false and hypocritical. When you are so used to hiding your abilities from others you hardly notice them yourself. Modestly, we push our successes to one side and dwell upon our failures. This is not going to help if you want to move forward and climb the ladders – all you'll do is slither down the snakes! !

It is important that you acknowledge your successes and reinforce your positive feelings. Each time you have a success, however small, write about it in your journal. Set yourself some of the goals I talked about in chapter 1 and which I will go into again in detail later. Each time you achieve a goal, celebrate! Do something simple like buying yourself a bar of chocolate or a bunch of flowers. Put a huge tick in your journal. Tell your mum or your best friend of your progress. Each step is important – a milestone in fact.

Consciously compliment yourself for some specific attributes. Are you hardworking, caring, loving, sensitive? Are you a good mother/father? Have you a quirky sense of humour or a wicked sense of fun? Are you honest, gentle, kind? Self-denigration is an easy habit which is easy to slip into. It leads to internal mutiny. If you treated others with the contempt with which you treat yourself you would be very badly received. So begin by giving yourself at least as much praise as you do criticism; gradually you will feel the confidence rise within you.

Non-assertiveness is the negative outcome of having a low opinion of yourself. How do you rate your self-esteem? Most people can evaluate their own acts, thoughts, feelings and behaviour to some extent and can determine whether they are at the top or on the lower rungs of the ladder. How do you measure up in relation to upbringing, nationality, height, size, religion, speech, the way you dress, stand, eat and the way you treat others? Do you feel lacking in any area because of who and what you are? We all have some attributes that we think hold us back. But do they – really? By all means be realistic – of course there are limits. We are all different and are all capable of achieving, perhaps not everything but a lot of things. To find out about your own feelings of inferiority ask yourself the questions laid out in chapter 3.

How to Recognize Low Self-Esteem and Improve It

ARE YOU SHY?

Shyness, blushing and stumbling over words are indications that a person is suffering from low self-esteem. These are reactions that non-assertive people recognize in themselves as lack of confidence and they are the reactions they fear most – because they can be seen by others. They fear that their red face, trembling hands, and tearful eyes are an indication to everyone around them that they have lost control. The fear mounts, the blushing worsens, and the dregs of their confidence seem to drain away. If you are afraid to speak up in a group, walk into a room full of people or get up on the dance floor, then you may feel deep down inside that others may be laughing at you and that their opinion of you as a person will be lowered still more if you make even the slightest mistake.

You are afraid they will think you are stupid or ignorant. Sometimes shy people have been rejected by parents, teachers, or friends in the past and they cannot bear the thought of it happening again. Being filled with this kind of dread is the very opposite of being brimful of confidence. If you feel confident you take risks like these. You state your opinions. You walk into rooms full of strangers wondering who you are going to find interesting – not agonizing over what these people will think of you. You go on the dance floor, even if you can't dance well – because who really cares anyway? If this type of person makes a mistake and others laugh they just throw their heads back and laugh with them. They do not agonize over what others may or may not think about them – they are totally focused on their positive actions and are unconcerned, if not unaware, of the remote possibility of others being critical of their actions.

Blushing is caused by a rush of blood to the face. It makes you feel uncomfortable and your heart beats faster. As a consequence, more blood is pumped to the surface of your skin. It becomes most apparent on the face, upper chest and neck. Being shy is unproductive. It prevents you from making the kind of friends you would like. It stops you from standing up for your rights and doing many of the things you would love to do. However, I have seen shy people overcome their blushing almost overnight once they realize that other people are more concerned with their own self-image than what they think of them. The people they are afraid of most are actually worrying about what others think of *them*. Far from trying to decide whether you are worth making friends with, they are wondering if you would consider being friends with *them*.

Try a little experiment. Choose someone you see every morning, perhaps at a bus stop, in a newsagent's or on your way to work, someone you have never spoken to or even smiled at before. You may have decided not to smile first because you imagine the other person will think you are strange. This is your challenge. Give them a smile. The first time they may not smile back because THEY may be too shy. But the second time you smile, they will realize you are not smiling at them because they look odd but because you want to be friendly. They will probably smile back at you purely as a reflex. It really is as simple as that. Try it out tomorrow. What does it matter if no one smiles back?

If you try it out on a stranger you will have lost nothing. If anything, it's their loss. But 'smiles beget smiles'. Think how infectious laughter is - no matter that you 'know not why' - it is a subconscious reaction to humour.

Once you are able to smile at people, try another goal. Speak to them. Most shy people have one fear above all others - that their shyness will prevent them from getting a partner. So if you are single, choose someone at a party - but don't whatever you do complicate things by trying it out on someone you really do fancy! That's just asking for trouble - too many other emotions flying about for it to work properly! Just look your chosen stranger in the eye, smile and ask him or her something about him or herself. Everyone - male or female - is longing to be asked about themselves. Aren't you? Ask a simple question like: 'Where do you work?' 'Do you live nearby?' 'Do you work with Norma?'. Have a small store of follow-up questions and if the first fails, try the others. They are bound to bring some response in the end. The secret is to give the other person the feeling that you think they are fascinating. They will be so pleased to find someone to talk to that they will chatter away nineteen to the dozen and if you listen, concentrate and become absorbed in what they are saying you WILL forget your fears. Stop wondering what other people think of you and what you think of them, and you are well on your way to overcoming your shyness. If you can do this just once you will have taken another step up the assertiveness ladder. The remedy is always there for you to take. And once again imagine your success, try to experience in your mind just how it will feel when you achieve it - practise, practise, practise.

If you put yourself deliberately into situations you know you find difficult you will gradually learn to cope with them. Once you have overcome shyness with strangers you can try it out in other situations where you have been accustomed to difficulties. And don't forget to give yourself a pat on the back each time you succeed. Be positive about your blushing. Don't keep telling yourself that a particular situation is bound to make you blush.

Remind yourself that everyone feels anxious in some situations. You are no different. And start to believe that blushing doesn't have to be your natural reaction. Start recognizing the situations that make you blush and consciously slow down your breathing. Remember, fast breathing accelerates the heartbeat and causes you to blush more. When you feel the blush rise, don't mumble and rush out of the room to hide it. Work through it. If you feel safe enough, say, 'Isn't it silly, I always blush when I talk to new people' and laugh at yourself. They will probably say 'So do I'. Make yourself carry on with the conversation. The more you do it the easier it will become.

It may help to act out a situation you think you will find difficult. Go through an imaginary job interview or the first meeting with your boy or girlfriend's parents. Get a close friend to play the opposite role. The laughs you are bound to have will take the heat out of the situation.

And try to stop imagining that people aren't attracted to you because of what you look like. Eyes are drawn to very beautiful people it's true, but beauty is only skin deep. Just because people look at others who are good looking it doesn't mean these people are any better than you. Nor does it mean they are good to know. You can be a good and likeable person whether you are attractive or not. So if you think you look unattractive – make the best of yourself and then try to forget it. It really doesn't matter. You probably don't look any different from most other people. And the best beauty aid you can have is an air of confidence. Whatever the shape of their nose, their face or the colour of their hair a person who walks with head high radiates that indefinable something that men and women alike respond to – magnetism. This in itself equals a kind of beauty. Don't you agree?

DO YOU SQUIRM WHEN GIVEN COMPLIMENTS?

A rising blush and a self put-down are common reactions to compliments. I am sure you have realized by now that if you have problems with your self-esteem then naturally you will find it difficult to accept compliments. If you have been rejected at some crucial time in your life, been regularly put down by brothers or sisters, if you have not come up to your family's or your own expectations in some way or if you see yourself as plain or stupid, no compliment will ever ring true. You may hear all the compliments in the world and you will still feel bad about yourself. You will accept none of this praise from others until you begin to feel that you are an acceptable person. Self-effacement is debilitating, it colours your judgement. You will have begun to climb out of this quagmire only when you can begin to accept compliments easily, without embarrassment and admit that at least some of them are true.

A non-assertive person may react to a compliment by saying something like 'I don't think what I did was that good. Anyone could have done it'. The assertive person will say 'Well, thank you – it's good to be appreciated'. People who know you will take notice of this change in your reaction. It can be fun to watch their bemused expressions. Give it a whirl! Watch their response to your new, positive approach to receiving a compliment successfully.

Remember there's no rush. A little change at a time is easier to handle. However some people become so caught up by this exciting idea of change that they move very quickly. Others take one small step at a time. It doesn't matter at what speed you travel as long as you go on moving forward.

As you move up the ladder and your happiness increases, be prepared to risk the resentment of people who cannot bear seeing others happy and confident. Remember how it felt to feel like that too. But keep in your mind that others who are equally joyful and confident will begin to seek you out because you are a pleasure to be with. Soon your confidence and your assertiveness will begin to soar and you will emanate magnetism. People are always attracted by *joie de vivre*.

ARE YOU ALWAYS FINDING FAULT WITH OTHERS?

I expect you can easily think of half a dozen people, friends or professional people, who you imagine must be assertive because they are always giving their opinions about things. They are always spouting these opinions, disagreeing with other people and finding fault. But this behaviour often gives out false messages. The fault-finding person may be thought of as aggressive and overconfident but very often quite the opposite is true. In reality they are negative and their carping is indicative of uncertainty and lack of confidence in themselves.

The mother who is always telling her daughter she is no good; the boy who is always picking on his sister; the father who constantly nags his son and tells him he's hopeless; these unhappy people pick on the ones they love because they feel threatened by them. In some cases parents are so lacking in self-esteem themselves that they become jealous of the achievements and confidence of their children. These parents may appear tough and hard but beneath it all they are really very insecure. Jealous feelings rise up and prompt negative reactions. Parents compete for the love of a child, or mother and daughter compete for the love of father, and fathers fear their growing sons will be more successful, taller and more handsome. Mothers see their daughters attracting the attention they once did. It unnerves them and makes them feel inadequate. It is sad but true.

Jealousy and possessiveness are the typical emotions which reveal a sense of inferiority. The degree to which you feel threatened is a measure of the degree to which you are unsure of yourself. The passion and anger evoked by these painful feelings can make you behave in ways you never thought possible and frequently you are often unaware of the root of the problem. I will talk about jealousy in more detail later on.

ARE YOU AFRAID OF COMPETITION?

Are you scared to take part in games, from tiddlywinks to chess, in case you lose? Each game must have a winner and a loser. Each time you take part you risk losing. Competitive games can be very scary for people with low self-esteem. This trait is very common in men who have been brought up in a competitive environment, whether within the family, in an institution, or in the early schooling atmosphere.

These unhappy people are afraid of doing badly and fear that their value as an individual will be at stake. They fear being evaluated by others who may have more skill and knowledge of the game. They have insufficient feelings of self-worth to protect them if they do not win. They fear they will lose their credibility. Many people will never play a game of any kind because they fear failure. They imagine others will find them stupid or uninformed; they are petrified their ignorance will show. They take the game far too seriously and each time they lose, their pride gets further damaged. They may show their hurt by sulking or becoming aggressive. We have all encountered bad losers at some time. The overturning of card tables or the snapping in two of billiard cues are signs that the loser has a very low self-esteem. He takes the loss personally. It is not just a game to him but an estimation of his worth.

MUST YOU KEEP UP WITH THE JONESES?

People who feel they must 'keep up with the Joneses' and who constantly brag about their fast car, their posh house, their possessions, their clothes with designer labels and the amazing people they have met, are trying very hard to conform to some imaginary standard they have set for themselves.

Teenagers who won't be seen dead in trainers that do not have a particular manufacturer's name splashed all over them and those who wear their labels on the outside are showing their feelings of low self-esteem to the world. These people feel they are worthless unless they can prove they are as good or better than others by displaying the trappings of trendiness, success and wealth.

Before you jump on this bandwagon ask yourself how can a person be superior just because they wear a pair of designer shoes or expensive clothes? Ask yourself honestly if you feel others are better than you because they are on first-name terms with their bank manager or a local pop star. The answer has to be NO of course not. These things have nothing to do with a person's own personal worth. Yet there are few people who do not use things like these as criteria for judging both.

There is nothing wrong with achieving and living well. There would be no point in becoming more assertive if it didn't help you to achieve some of your goals BUT if you think it makes you better than others – think again. Owning all these things only means you have acquired more wealth (or are trying to look as if you have) but no – DEFINITELY NOT – that you are a better human being. It will do little to enhance your self-esteem.

DO YOU ALWAYS HAVE TO BE NUMBER ONE?

The people who always have to be the best or the fastest or the strongest in every sphere are the saddest people of all. They take their whole life far too seriously and may often become stressed because the constant striving is detrimental to their basic wellbeing. They ultimately become the personification of discontent – and it shows! They think that every time they win a game, get to the front of the traffic queue, make someone else look small, or win an argument, they are making themselves look more important. But always being the best is a pain in the neck to others. Ordinary people who make mistakes and joke about them are much more fun to be with. The saddest part of all is that while these people, who think they are superior, are trying so hard to prove that they are wonderful in every area they are actually broadcasting to the whole world that they are really insecure and that they have a very poor opinion of themselves. In the long run, instead of these successes making them popular, and sought after by other people, they do the opposite. They drive away the people they so desperately want to admire them, so ultimately the outcome is self-defeating.

Sometimes, to keep feeling 'number one' these sad people feel they must hit out at others. It is hard to acknowledge this in ourselves but it is true that many of us find that we are behaving just like them because we have unconsciously picked up behavioural traits from those who once damaged or hurt us. Things that we have learned *can* be unlearned. If you feel that this might lie behind your difficulties seek some professional counselling help. It is not easy to unhook yourself from roles picked up in young vulnerable years and to look at your more negative traits, like scoring over others, being possessive, demanding, taunting and controlling. If we have experienced humiliation when we were young we will do anything to escape it in later life. If the thing we fear most, from experience, is the caustic comment or the sardonic attitude, we may use these weapons against someone we see as 'weak'. Those treated cruelly in their youth may compensate by being very kind, trying to make up for the hurt they suffered, but for others the reaction is to act cruelly in return. In hurting others they are re-enacting what they have had done to them and saving themselves from experiencing that vulnerability.

ARE YOU AFRAID OF MAKING MISTAKES?

Many believe the myth that it is okay for children to look awkward or foolish but that adults must never falter. This is absolute rubbish. Flexibility and the desire to learn are all-important. 'MAKING MISTAKES IS THE KEY TO MAKING PROGRESS.' Remember, negative feedback assists you to reach your goal if you let it. If you want to change you must allow yourself some awkwardness to start with. It is like learning to ride a bike. You may fall off a few times but practice makes perfect. It is experience that counts. Find your own speed and push yourself off – gently. Don't let that inner voice destroy your balance and convince you that you 'can't'. Nothing ventured, nothing gained.

ARE YOU ALWAYS APOLOGIZING?

Too many apologies are a common characteristic in those who feel inferior. Those who are constantly asking to be forgiven or excused even for minor errors of judgement are clear candidates.

Apologies are often necessary but they can become annoying when repeated. The person who collides with you as you are about to cross a road or knocks into you with shopping is a common example. People with these feelings of inferiority often apologize even before you realize what has happened. The person who backs down in a conversation with a humble apology when someone more forceful has interrupted (sometimes rudely) and who often begins sentences with 'I'm terribly sorry to trouble you but. . .', 'I'm probably wrong but. . .', and 'I know this will probably sound stupid but. . .' are pre-empting criticism before it even arises. They don't seem to realize that when they voice these constant apologies and self put-downs, they are announcing to everyone that they so often feel in the wrong and make so many mistakes that they are advertising their self-effacement. These unfortunate people are accustomed to being treated as if they are ineffectual so of course it becomes easy for them and for others to maintain the impression.

People who feel totally inadequate, even in everyday situations, begin to believe that they are failures as human beings and if they are criticized for even the smallest thing they feel devastated. You see their hangdog expression, the hurt look in their eye, the embarrassed blush and eyes that fill with tears at the least provocation. Sometimes it is painful to watch them.

Yet if someone feels good about themselves they see criticism as a mere blip on the screen of life. It is constructive, something that they can learn from and something they will try not to allow to happen again – and even if it does – so what? They'll try again, and again. They will keep going – their determination to do something, to get somewhere or to achieve their goal is their purpose. They think positively. If people are 'comfortable' with mistakes they welcome the opportunity of trying something new, of taking those risks even if they know they might make a pig's ear of it. They know deep down that they will learn from the experience. If they didn't attempt it in the first place they would never learn anything. This fear of failure holds back so many capable people. Again, negative feedback actually assists you in achieving your goal.

CHAPTER 4

Problems With Love and Sex

ARE YOU AFRAID TO BE ASSERTIVE WITH THE ONE YOU LOVE?

Love and sex have attracted more attention on our bookshelves, in the media or anywhere else, than almost any other subject in recent years. Songs, films, books and sermons are constantly proclaiming the joys and sorrows caused by this, the most powerful of our feelings.

Among all the components of a loving relationship, intimacy is probably the quality most longed for. It is the culmination of all our hopes and desires, the supreme goal for which we have yearned and its elusiveness increases our desire to attain it. However, it is frequently the most fugitive of our goals. Without assertiveness it becomes difficult, and sometimes impossible, to find. One of the key characteristics of closeness is acceptance of another person. It is vital, too, to be able to expose your inadequacies to your partner, in the knowledge that they will be accepted along with everything else. An assertive person is not worried about showing his or her vulnerability and is more able to accept inadequacies in others. From acceptance grows trust. Once you begin to accept one another for what you are, you start to rely on each other. It is important that you believe your partner will not betray your trust.

ARE YOU AFRAID TO BE ASSERTIVE IN THE BEDROOM?

This section is primarily aimed at women but it can certainly apply to men too. So please read on. It is always important to have a broad view.

Do you feel let down after lovemaking? Are you getting the kind of loving you want? Does your partner do all the little things you dream he will do or do you lie there waiting for him to guess what it is that rings your bell? If you feel that this sums up your situation, can you work out why it happens? Maybe you find it difficult to ask for what you want. It can be quite scary to use sexual words for the first time – it takes a little practice. Maybe you feel it would be selfish to ask for what you want. Maybe you've been programmed only to give and you find taking difficult. Maybe you think your partner is lazy, selfish or too inexperienced, or maybe there is some buried resentment which is stopping you from letting go. You may be telling yourself 'If he loved me he ought to know how to please me'. Or do you sometimes pluck up the courage to ask for that special stroke or to suggest making love in your favourite position ONLY when you feel your partner 'owes' you? Are you always thinking about ways to please your partner, putting your needs last?

Women frequently have the greatest difficulty in asking for what they would like in bed. They may feel it is wrong to take any sort of lead. They may think it's not 'ladylike' to take the initiative. Many have been brought up to feel guilty about enjoying sexual pleasure and have never really listened to their own bodies. They've never even found out what their bodies need in order to respond. If they can overcome all the negative reasons, they may find that taking responsibility for the joint satisfaction of the union is a powerful aphrodisiac both to themselves and their partners.

Next time you make love observe your own responses and make some mental notes on what you would like and what you need to make you feel good.

Be specific. What kind of stimulation do you want, where, and for how long? Some people focus on what their partner is doing to get a buzz, others need fantasies to stimulate themselves.

No matter how much you are loved and cared for, no matter how close you are to your partner, there is no way he or she can read your mind. Your partner cannot know your body as well as you do. Both partners need verbal feedback to know how they are doing. If your partner is touching you somewhere you don't like, just moving his hand away is not enough. If you don't tell him you don't like what he is doing he will assume you do – and keep doing it! You will grow increasingly resentful and sex will lose its sparkle. It doesn't mean your partner doesn't love you. It doesn't mean he doesn't want to please you or that he is being selfish. He simply doesn't know. Let him in on your secrets. Whisper the words in his ear if you can't say them out loud. Let your partner know where your sensitive places are – introduce something new each time you make love. Repeat your requests if he seems to have forgotten and when he's got it right introduce some more.

Instead of letting your thoughts wander off on work problems, the kids and household tasks, focus on positive things about your partner. Think about the strong muscles that are tensing and relaxing in his thighs, think about the gentle way he touches you with those strong hands, think about his rhythmic movements, his tight bottom and enjoy the pleasure that is written on his face. If you enjoy his excitement as well as your own, your pleasure will increase and your partner will be overjoyed at your input. If you are constantly thinking about how to please your partner at the expense of your own enjoyment you will both miss out. Making sure you get turned on in the way you like is another way of giving pleasure to the man or woman in your life. You are NOT being selfish. You'd both get more out of it if you stopped being so overwhelmingly giving and took a little joy for yourself now and again. No one

- absolutely no one - is totally aware of their partner when they reach the higher pleasure levels. Very often the only awareness is of oneself. Becoming absorbed in your own pleasure can be the ultimate turn-on for your partner. He will adore bringing you to a place 'out of this world'.

However, men and women who are overly concerned for their partners make inefficient lovers. They are so busy trying to stimulate, excite and switch on their partner's pleasure zones that they can't respond as they should. It almost becomes a clinical operation. You can overdo the loving by trying too hard to get it right. An assertive lover who really enjoys his or her own body is a sexy lover. Two assertive people who give and take, and who allow themselves to enjoy their own pleasure, have all the ingredients for a happy and successful sex life.

Most of the space in my agony column is devoted to the sadness and even heartbreak caused by love or the lack of it. It certainly does seem to make the world go round for some people and causes it to come to a dead halt for others. And it is not only the young who write of their emotional or sexual problems either. Similar problems continue to distress older and retired people, even those in their eighties and more. In affairs of the heart we don't seem to learn in the way we do in other areas of life. The same jealousies and insecurities that dog us as teenagers appear to follow us in later years and unless we make a concentrated effort to change our reactions and make the changes necessary to improve this important aspect of our lives we will never know the true joys that it can bring.

Some years ago when I was working as a nurse on a medical ward, I talked to an elderly gentleman who had been admitted with chest pain. I found him crying quietly to himself one night. When I sat beside him to find out what was troubling him, he told me he was afraid his seventy-two-year-old wife would be unfaithful with his neighbour while he was in hospital. I felt really sorry for him. Nothing I could say could reassure him. And from what he told me jealousy and the overwhelming feeling that he was not as good as other men had spoiled most of his life. I imagine it had spoiled his wife's life too. Here they were, in their twilight years, still suffering the same fears and insecurities they did when they were young. Even the fact that they'd been together so long had done nothing to reassure this man that his wife was not going to run off with someone else.

Lack of communication had not helped the problem over the years. If they had been able to express their thoughts and feelings to each other, there would have been no need for this additional burden in his present situation - their problem had only aged with them.

It is a fact that each one of us has a slightly different idea of what real love is all about. How on earth we expect a relationship to run smoothly goodness only knows - yet each time we fall in love we hope that it will. There is a much better chance of working things out if you take assertive skills seriously and apply them to your nearest and dearest, instead of just doing what comes naturally and following your instincts - instincts which can be very destructive. Be positive. Set yourself a goal - write about it in your journal - imagine your success in whichever area you wish to improve and practise it over and over again in your mind until you have perfected it well enough to try out on the world at large.

MYTHS

There are lots of myths associated with true love. Different cultures, different religions and even different families have varying ideas about how we should behave within a loving and close relationship.

So in order to achieve a successful relationship we must find a way through the minefield of myths and powerful emotions that lies behind our behaviour.

We hear the myths surrounding love and sex reaffirmed every day in romantic songs. We read about them in magazines and in the myriad novels from Jane Austen to the romantic paperbacks of Barbara Cartland currently cramming the shelves in our bookstores. They all perpetuate the widespread and irrational idea that we as humans NEED love and that without it we are nothing. But is this really true? Let us look at one or two of these myths more closely.

Myth 1. You are nobody if nobody loves you

It would seem, if you were to believe the lyrics of countless songs we hear, that you really are nobody if nobody loves you. But of course this is not true. Many successful people from Mother Teresa to Cliff Richard, from Greta Garbo to Albert Schweitzer, have proved that life can be a triumph without being in love the whole time.

Sure, in many people's minds the ideal union – the very top rung of the ladder – is a lifetime spent with one special person with whom they have a trusting, caring and supportive relationship; a partnership built upon total honesty, complete understanding and intimacy which fulfils their dreams of living happily ever after. However, this is one of the most difficult things to achieve. Some of the unhappiest people I have come across are living in a sham marriage with a partner for whom their feelings died long ago. Even fairytale royal marriages can end in disaster, as we all know. To my mind, the alternative to an unhappy marriage is being happily single. Once you get used to it single life can become so attractive that it becomes very difficult to relinquish. It is possible to reclaim yourself and live your own life as you want to live it without being attached to someone else in an exclusive relationship.

Single people can achieve their individual potential. And living alone, with its many opportunities for self-expression and fulfilment, is summed up by many in one word – 'Freedom'. Yet others give the impression they are living a life that is second best and some even feel they have to apologize for their single state.

Myth 2. If you don't feel jealous it can't be real love

Many people feel that the jealous feelings which surface when their partner is paying attention to someone else are a sign of their deep love.

However, the green-eyed monster is the most common trouble spot in relationships. For some, the feelings can be tossed aside – you may be amazed to discover that some people can get a thrill from their partner being desired by someone else, but for others it causes not only unhappiness but panic, anger and sometimes illness.

In some rare instances people can become so depressed that they become seriously ill through jealousy. Just as surely as someone can die from a broken heart - so jealousy can bring about premature death. These sad people do sometimes succeed in taking their own life. Jealousy is the greatest spoiler of happiness I know - such a futile emotion.

JEALOUSY

It is not just the jealous partner who suffers from the obsessive fear and sick feeling that sometimes takes over a person's life. The victim's happiness is destroyed too and the ripple-effect can pass through the whole family and even extend into social situations spoiling friendships and business relationships. One jealous lady who wrote to me actually walked into a board meeting at her husband's office, in a frenzy of jealousy. Dramatically, she accused him of sleeping with his secretary because she'd found a cheque stub in his pocket with the name of a florist near his place of work. She had put two and two together and, believing the worst, decided to do something about it. She was wrong - hopelessly wrong. He had paid for flowers to decorate a table for a business meeting, when the catering staff had omitted to do it. Her husband was understandably embarrassed. It was the last straw in a whole string of unreasonable actions on her behalf and, ultimately, he could take no more and he divorced her.

A jealous person may be possessive and demanding, dictating the other person's actions to such a degree that it makes life intolerable. A usually gentle soul can become violent and destructive, upsetting the mental and physical well-being of everyone they love and, as happened in the saga of the business meeting, can end up destroying the very thing they want most of all.

There are, of course, times when jealousy may be quite understandable. Rational jealousy has been with the human race since the day of the cave man. It is to do with survival. If you have an ongoing relationship with someone you love, someone whom you have cared for and who has cared for you for a period of time and without whom you feel life would be intolerable, obviously the fear of losing him or her and the good life you share, threatens your future, your life style, and your general well-being – it threatens your very existence. If the person involved is disrupting your relationship by seeing someone else or threatening to leave, then no one could expect you to sit back calmly and let it carry on. In situations like these you can legitimately claim to feel angry and disappointed.

You can tell your partner how deeply you have been hurt and shed as many tears as you like. But one thing you must never do is to transfer unnecessary blame to yourself. There is life after the break-up of a relationship but if you have a low feeling of self-worth this will set you back even further and in so doing, have a detrimental effect on your future.

Irrational jealousy is something completely different. It causes serious anxiety, anger and depression. It eats into your very soul, destroying love and putting relationships of all kinds at risk. Sufferers often spend hours just speculating where their partner is. They go over and over a list of the women he knows and imagine he is with one, then another, and imagines what they're doing together. These women hunt in pockets, briefcases and desk drawers for signs of infidelity and in extreme cases they have phones tapped and enlist the help of friends. They may even hire private detectives to follow the partner in the hope of uncovering some compromising situations. These people have the most serious problem.

Before you stray into the quicksand of irrational jealousy stop and give yourself a good talking to. Remind yourself that you cannot put your partner under lock and key. No one is going to be happy if their freedom is taken away from them, however much you love them.

What you must do in these circumstances is have your own set of stock statements written out in your journal to read out loud to yourself every time you feel the green-eyed monster clawing its way up inside you. You can invent your own phrases, of course, but here are a few examples.

- I love my partner very much. If he leaves me or fancies someone else I would hate it. I would be angry and unhappy – but I would continue to like and accept myself unconditionally even if he did.
- I love my partner very much. I want no one else but he is not obliged to love me in return.
- If my partner treated me inconsiderately or unfairly I would try to understand why he did it. I would try to talk to him about it and persuade him to be more loving.

If you can start to think along these lines you will save yourself needless emotional turmoil. It does work, I promise you. The first time I made a conscious effort to stop my own jealous feelings in their tracks – and succeeded – I felt elated.

My partner was chatting to a very attractive girl. Instead of staring at him and trying to burn an imaginary hole in the back of his head, I turned away. It was not easy. I ran over my stock of anti-jealousy phrases in my head and started to talk to the nearest man I could find. It wasn't long before my partner had left the girl and was by my side. This quick turn of my head had saved me a whole evening's irrational anger and both of us a needless argument.

Sufferers from irrational jealousy truly believe that they need their partner's total love and attention at all times. They feel that if a partner falls out of love with them or becomes attracted to someone else it only goes to prove that they really are unlovable and worthless. Sadly they often drive their partner away. It is completely self-defeating. All it does is to emphasize the jealous person's own poor self-image and the burning need to be loved just escalates. They can become extremely low and desperate. Don't allow this to happen to you.

The fact is that no one can guarantee to love anyone else indefinitely. If you need these guarantees you are asking for the impossible. You are bound to end up being miserable and probably alone. If a jealous person does find someone who makes them the centre of their universe and if this someone goes along with their wishes by refusing to meet other people or to having few – if any – experiences outside their own relationship life will hold few joys. So either way they lose out and someone else's quality of life is reduced too.

The jealous person must ask him- or herself if wanting to own someone totally makes good sense. Sure it's great to strive to create and maintain an exclusive relationship with the one you love. It's what most people would like to achieve, but you won't get it by demanding, by playing private detectives or by causing unpleasant scenes. It goes back to the original concept of assertiveness – the first rung of the ladder. The first rule is that you must learn to like and accept yourself unconditionally as you are. Then you will be much more likely to find someone who will care for you in return. However, if you can only think yourself worthy if you are bathed in someone else's love and can accept yourself conditionally upon somebody else's opinions of you, then you don't have the remotest chance of achieving your goal.

In every area where lack of assertiveness lies behind relationship breakdown, self-liking and self-acceptance become the keys to the door that leads towards your assertive future. When jealousy seems to be tearing your lives apart a lack of these traits is certainly at the root of the problem, and if this book does nothing more than make you think about ways to improve your self-esteem then it will have achieved a great deal. Being irrationally jealous will almost certainly create a lot of emotional misery within any intimate liaison. The end result is either a destroyed relationship or a boring one where neither of you has any outside interests, occupations or friends.

CHAPTER 5

Work Problems

ASSERTIVENESS IN THE WORKPLACE

Being assertive in the great big world of business is the key to promotion and to good relationships with superiors and colleagues alike. However, before we can begin to think about being assertive at work we must first of all get that job.

UNEMPLOYMENT

Being unemployed can be soul-destroying. It can easily push someone already lacking in confidence and assertiveness further down the slippery slope of hopelessness. It can make a person feel helpless, trapped and doubtful of climbing out of the miserable circle of poverty. For the unemployed a daily purpose is a must – whether it is a routine for checking the newspapers for jobs, the job centre itself, the local shops, or offices and factories. Without a plan your day can so easily lose its shape. There's nothing to make you leap out of bed bright-eyed and bushy-tailed. You can't help wondering if life will always be this way. Unless you can keep on reminding yourself that the situation is not your fault and that being out of work doesn't make you a worthless person, you will begin to slide. Don't let this happen. You must keep trying. Follow every lead, answer every appropriate ad. Don't be despondent. It only takes one of those prospective employers to say 'yes – please come and work for me' for things to change dramatically.

Carry the tips you will find in my chapter on body language and communication skills in your head when you attend interviews. Believe in yourself and your abilities. Have one of those conversations with your mirror image that affirms your feelings of self-worth. Tell yourself once more what you are good at and what you are capable of and walk out of your front door with your head held high. Remember there's nothing as attractive as confidence – even if it is assumed for the occasion. Unless you have confidence it is difficult for others to see you in a positive light. Remember that most people underestimate themselves but they don't let the rest of the world know it. They convince themselves that all is well and they win. So without seeming to 'show off', aim to be firm when putting your views and your personality across. The act of convincing yourself becomes such a smooth process that it becomes completely believable to others. So think positively. Set your goal. Imagine in your mind that you are successful, confident and attractive – you will begin to feel it. Practise, practise, practise!

You must keep telling yourself that you are the best person for the job. Believe it with all your heart. You wouldn't have applied if you didn't think you could handle it. Look at other prospective interviewees and see for yourself that they look no more able to do the job than you.

Get some practice by getting some unemployed friends together and play the role of interviewer and interviewee. Some useful questions to try out are:

- 'Tell me about yourself.'
- 'What hobbies do you have?'
- 'What are your strengths?'
- 'What are your weaknesses?'
- 'Why do you want this job?'

Swap ideas. Find something positive to say about yourself in each answer. And don't offer derogatory information such as bad habits or failings when asked about your weaknesses. Say things like 'I'm a bit of a workaholic', not that you are lazy and spend too much time in bed! Say you're a perfectionist, not that you are untidy or boring. There's no need to tell whoppers. Try to press the good points you really do have – otherwise you may spend wasted hours worrying about living up to the false standards you may have set yourself – that is what un-assertive people often do. Think positively. Think of the end of a past interview where you had a good feeling and analyse why. Do the same for an unsuccessful interview and discover what made you dissatisfied with the outcome.

After each interview write a diary about what went on. List the questions you were asked and what your answers were. Think about how you could improve those answers next time.

Learn something from each interview. They are never wasted experiences. Don't allow yourself to get disheartened if you don't get the first or even the tenth job. Keep telling yourself 'It is not my fault and I am worth employing'. It only needs one affirmative reply and you are on your way. I know you need a lot of courage to persist – but it does pay off. Remember 'Courage is a virtue – it makes all other virtues possible'.

Where else can you go, be the centre of attention and talk for half an hour or so, all about yourself? It is better than going to an analyst and it's cheaper!

CHAPTER 6

How to Deal with Rejection, Criticism and Blame

ARE YOU AFRAID OF REJECTION?

Dealing with rejection is a difficult area. It is never easy to take rejection – even for the most confident among us. However, if you accept yourself as you are when others disagree with you or dislike you, you will not be destroyed, in the way that those with lower self-esteem can be. People who are lacking in confidence feel the only way they can be successful and respected is for other people to agree with them and even admire them. They feel emotional pain if they don't. If you are to learn assertiveness skills you must ask yourself why on earth you should put the value you have of yourself in the hands of others. If you don't agree with others and if you imagine they don't like you or are showing signs of not accepting you, it only means that you don't fit in with that particular group. It does not mean that you are totally unlikeable. Are you beginning to understand these different ways of looking at yourself? New, positive thoughts will eventually become the building blocks of the new, assertive you.

Some people cannot even introduce themselves to others

because they fear rejection. They cannot muster the confidence to voice their opinion even amongst friends in case someone disagrees, and they refuse to go to parties or to do anything where they think they might be compared with others. Can you see how destructive these feelings can be and how shallow their lives will become if they allow it to continue?

In order to deal with the feelings of rejection that cause your self-esteem to sink, you must first understand that there is nothing to be afraid of if you are spurned or rejected. It does not mean that you are no good at keeping the love of a man or a woman. It does not mean you are useless in everything you do or that you will be rejected by a different group of people.

CONFLICT

Are you Afraid of Conflict?

One of the greatest impediments or blocks in trying to create a successful relationship at school, at work or within a personal relationship, is an inability to face conflict. Conflict occurs in all close relationships. Since we are all different from each other it is inevitable that any two people will find themselves in conflict at some time or other. Conflict is just a difference in what two people want, need or think. You want to plan the new décor for the sitting room, your partner wants to make love. You want to go for a walk, your partner wants to watch TV. You think children should go to boarding school, your partner hates the idea.

Marianne and Nicholas had been battling for years over the way to bring up their children. After having only six months of counselling they started to understand that each had good reasons for behaving in the way they did. After ten years of marriage they began really to get to know each other. They became interested in why they behaved in certain ways and why they wanted their children to be treated in a certain manner. They explored what they wanted for their children and from where these ideas emanated. Did their parents have similar expectations? Why did they get angry in certain situations? Why wouldn't Nicholas read books on childcare? Why did he get angry when Marianne did? They asked questions of each other about their own parents' expectations of them. As they worked their way through the reasons behind certain behaviour traits they were able to make changes and accept compromises more easily and act accordingly.

Facing conflict in a loving relationship is an opportunity to change patterns learnt in childhood which are inappropriate in adult life. Most of us still react to conflict in the same way we reacted as children. Being open with your partner is the only way to unlearn these patterns and unblock these impediments. There is a time to stop blaming others and to take responsibility for our own lives, to take risks like being vulnerable and admitting pain, and building the kind of relationship we want together.

Here are some questions which might help break through the barriers:

- Why is my partner behaving in this way?
- Do I feel angry, afraid or annoyed?
- Why should this be happening?
- What personal issues does my partner stir in me?
- Why is it so important for me to get my own way?
- Why does my partner always have to be right?
- How does my reaction to his disagreement affect him?
- What fears lay behind my feeling threatened?
- Why does my partner's attitude affect me this way?

Conflicts occur over a mulitude of differences but it's not the cause of the conflict but the handling of it that matters. The difficulty lies in how each partner copes with disagreement.

ARE YOU AFRAID OF CRITICISM?

There are bound to be areas in which you are more sensitive than others. In these situations even the most assertive person will feel emotions rise up. Our sensitive areas – the buttons that are pressed by others – are very individual, intimate and private. They may be due to embarrassment about our size, our accent, our colour, our financial state, our sexuality or any other personal qualities. Everyone has these sensitive areas. But other people have no way of knowing what they are. If someone mentions something that brings up hurtful feelings within you the chances are that it is purely accidental. They have no idea of the pain they have caused. This is where you need to speak out.

Painful feelings which stem from childhood experiences of rejection and disapproval overwhelm you. Criticism we received then may also have been accompanied by feelings of guilt. The legacy of these experiences stays with us and even as adults we experience echoes of childhood pain. We often see criticism as loss of someone's affection, hurt pride and loss of self-esteem. It is very painful.

This is not something that you will be able to cure overnight. However, you can begin to take the sting out of it a little by sorting out criticism which is valid from that which is not.

Valid Criticism

This is criticism that you know is fair. You really weren't concentrating and you did get your facts wrong. You have been bad-tempered lately. You did forget to do whatever it was your boss asked and you did turn up late twice last week. Learn to accept that criticism is only aimed at a specific aspect of your behaviour. It is not aimed at you as a person. You are not a forgetful person – you forgot to do what you were asked today – that's all. You are not a bad-tempered person. You have been short-tempered lately (there's usually a reason). You were late. You get things wrong sometimes – we all do. It is human to make mistakes. No one is perfect. Agree with the criticism, apologize and forget it. This is just another learning experience.

Invalid Criticism

Invalid criticism is often handed out by those who want to put you down. Don't just accept it, all the time wondering if there is in fact some truth in it. Ask yourself if the criticism is generally true of you.

If not, then you must renounce it. If you cannot bring yourself to say it out loud at least tell yourself that 'This is NOT true. It is unfair to judge me on one example. Generally my work is very good'.

If you feel panic rising when you are criticized remember it is a legacy you have carried around since childhood. Remind yourself frequently that making mistakes doesn't make you a useless person. It means you have made a few mistakes, that's all! But you must also remember this in your treatment of others and understand their reactions if your remarks appear to be excessive. As you begin to understand yourself more you inevitably begin to understand others better too and you will stop making wild assumptions about them or their behaviour.

If you accept criticism as valid, say so. If your boss reprimands you for dealing with a situation in an inappropriate manner, say 'I agree, I shouldn't have lost my temper with Mr Smith'. If you want to say 'sorry' do so but then leave it. Don't grovel and don't go on about it. Try not to mention it again.

If you want to take it further to see how things could be improved you could add 'How would you suggest I put things right? – I'd appreciate your guidance'.

Are you Afraid to Criticize Others?

Does the thought of criticizing someone else fill you with dread? Do you imagine they will be totally devastated and what's more do you imagine that they will immediately stop liking you? If criticism is painful for you to accept then nine times out of ten it will be just as painful for you to criticize others. The same feelings of shame and hurt pride well up inside you as you imagine how they will feel, and very often you retreat. You take the blame yourself because it seems easier.

However it is possible to give criticism without inflicting pain. When it is your turn to criticize, remember it is the behaviour you are criticizing and not the person.

Instead of saying 'You are a complete idiot for doing that!' say you weren't happy with the way something was handled. Instead of saying 'You are an untidy child' say 'Your room is messy – I want you to do something about it'. Instead of saying

'You are a wicked boy' say 'That was a really unkind thing to say to Grandma'. Instead of saying 'You are clumsy' say 'That was a clumsy thing to do'. Get the picture?

One way to give criticism is to remove the sting by first reminding the person you are to criticize of his or her good points: 'I'm very pleased with the way you handle clients, Joe. These letters are great too, but please, you must start coming in on time in the mornings.'

Giving praise softens the blow. So always try to say something positive before you weigh in with the criticism. If the person you are criticizing feels valued by you, your criticism is more likely to be accepted without loss of self-esteem.

Make concise and constructive requests. Vague references to the amount of work in your in tray and how no one else seems to do anything are not enough. Don't drop hints about how overworked Tim is and how no one offers to help him. You should make your requests clear.

For example: 'The batch of letters you typed were excellent. Thanks. When you've had your tea break would you take some time to help Tim with the post? He's snowed under.'

Never assume that people can read your mind. They probably are not aware of the effect their behaviour is having on you. If someone is annoying you, for example by interrupting your conversation, don't fly off the handle when they do it yet again. Wait. Then, calmly and without hostility in your voice, say 'When you interrupt me like that I feel that what I have just said is worthless – please try not to do it'. Or even in a light-hearted way suggest it is now your turn to take the floor.

In your journal I want you to start listing jobs you must tackle during the next week. Under the heading CRITICISM give yourself a job to do. Think of someone who has been upsetting you for some time and whom you have been afraid to confront.

Think about ways to apply this strategy to the situation and let the person know how you feel in a way that is constructive and easier for them to accept than the sort of attack you fear. When you have thought about what you want to say practise your first attempts in front of a mirror, or record your attempts on a tape recorder. Listen to yourself and how your words sound and keep practising until you can speak the words calmly and non-aggressively – in a friendly way, even. Then when you are ready – go for it. And when it's done put another large tick in your journal.

Children who hear themselves constantly described as lazy, wicked, stupid, rude, may consciously or subconsciously absorb this criticism and eventually begin to believe they ARE these things. Instead of seeing these expressions as criticisms of behaviour which can be changed, they see it as a criticism of their entire self and their feelings of self-worth plummet. Their attitude becomes negative and they actually anticipate always being in the wrong. So the 'positive thinking syndrome' is put into action.

Children constantly given bad messages about themselves feel hurt and rejected. They want to stand up for themselves but they daren't. These frustrations build up and when as adults, they are criticized, these feelings rise to the surface and they may over-react. They feel criticized as people and not for the simple mistake they may have made. Remember it is the 'event' which must be criticized and not the person.

My final word on the subject of criticism is to always try to end conversations which have involved some criticism on a positive note. This is particularly important if there has been a long discussion and there is a risk of hurt pride. It is often helpful to touch a person lightly in some way – either by shaking their hand or just touching their shoulder or forearm and saying something like 'I'm really glad we've had this talk. It is good to clear the air because I do value your opinions.' I will go into the value of touching and how you can voice your requests in more assertive ways by using body language, in detail, later on.

BLAME

Placing blame is a necessary part of life. In many human situations it is appropriate to attribute effects to causes. Which organization placed the bomb on the plane? Who started the fight? Who murdered President Kennedy? Examples are endless. Every national and international disaster confirms our need to apportion blame to make sense of the horrors in this world. It establishes a logical framework in which to live.

However, there are many occasions where blaming others becomes a way of life. It is a way of people denying – particularly to themselves – that anything that goes wrong is ever their fault. They fear losing face by owning up to what they have done. They want to avoid the pain of admitting mistakes in order to preserve their own self-image.

There are others who go to the opposite extreme and bear responsibility for almost everything that goes wrong for fear of confronting others and for the sake of keeping the peace. They may want to keep their reputation for being unselfish and kind, or hope to garner warmth and sympathy from others.

(There are also, of course, the more difficult circumstances where people try to blame others in order to hurt or humiliate them or to ruin their reputation. These are potentially volatile situations where the intent is quite malicious and are due to much more complicated issues.)

False innocence and false guilt are at opposite ends of the blame spectrum. There are those who collide with someone in the supermarket who yell 'Look where you're going' to the embarrassed shopper, and others who apologize instinctively before they've even had time to work out whose fault it was. People who are consumed with false guilt can feel entirely responsible for the happiness of their whole family and whenever anything at all goes wrong they are always the ones who feel guilty.

Do you ever find yourself either blaming others for things that go wrong or constantly finding yourself taking the blame yourself in order to avoid an argument? Both ways of avoiding confrontation can evoke deep-seated feelings of guilt and oppression. If you can, begin to sort out honestly what is your fault, and what is not. If you can, begin to stand up to those who blame you and if you can, admit your own mistakes and take responsibility for them. You will discover a new sense of pride and self-regard. It just takes a little more thought and some careful planning.

In order to begin to change your reactions you must first become more aware of the games people play when placed in 'blaming' situations. We have all experienced the pain of being blamed for something we did not do. Being blamed unfairly evokes feelings of humiliation, unfairness, anger and resentment.

Most people play the blaming game at some time or another but if you are to become truly assertive you must become more aware of these hidden games that are played during conversations which include blame.

Double standards operate in everyday life. They are played out in safe ways every day at football matches. Crowds of people will shout 'Foul' when a member of their team is attacked but when their team member is guilty they look aghast and say 'The ref must be on something!' People tend to see what they want to see. It is an extremely obvious example of 'positive thinking', but used in this way, it is unhelpful to anyone, 'blamer' or 'blamed'.

How many people do you know who call drivers who exceed the speed limit to overtake, 'Maniacs', when they regularly do the same thing? Similar scenarios are played out in slightly more injurious ways in the workplace and in the home.

Both the person who takes the blame for things they did not do and the one who blames others to save face need to become conscious of what they do. As you begin to be more aware of the ways you handle 'blaming' situations, own up to your journal. No one is going to read it but you. Write down the dialogue of conversations roughly as you remember them and think of ways in which you could have handled the situations differently. Write down your new reaction and say them out loud, using your tape recorder if you wish. It's a little like rewriting the script of a play.

Practise your statements over and over until you feel comfortable with them and then go out and try them on the world. Here are some phrases you could use.

- 'I don't accept that I am responsible for what happened.'

- 'I refuse to be treated as a scapegoat.'
- 'When you try to make me responsible for your mistakes I feel really resentful.'
- 'I refuse to accept the blame for this.'
- 'Nobody made you do this. You chose to.'
- 'Why do you find it so difficult to accept that it was your decision?'

- 'I'm sorry.'
- 'I apologize.'
- 'That was my fault.'
- 'I accept responsibility for that.'
- 'Yes that mistake was mine.'
- 'It was me. You are not to blame.'
- 'Please accept my apologies.'

List the phrases that you feel will be most helpful in your journal and give yourself another tick when you have used them in a real-life situation. And give yourself a great big pat on the back. It is not easy to change habits of a lifetime. Changing this one thing is a huge step up the ladder; a positive step towards attaining your new assertive self.

CHAPTER 7

About Making Changes

STRATEGIES FOR GROWTH

List some wants in your journal.

- I want to marry Mary.
- I want a house with a garden.
- I want to make love on a beach.
- I want to be a writer.
- I want to learn to sail.
- I want to go dancing.

Now you must start your plan of action. Get yourself an exercise book in which to make notes and plot your progress. Put up a notice board on which you will write your goals and objectives so you can follow your own progress in assertiveness.

Ask yourself what your emotional needs are and write them down. Make a list of the things that are important to you. No one else will see your book, so don't feel embarrassed. If nothing comes to mind quickly because you have been so used to blocking out your needs, make some guesses. Keep your journal by your bedside – or under the mattress – in case inspiration comes when you are in bed.

- Whom would you like to love you?
- What kind of work would you like to do?
- What kind of home would you like to live in?
- What kind of fun do you really enjoy?
- Where would you like to make love?

You may find that when you really search your mind for these things and realize just how much you are not getting, you are hurting more than you imagined.

Like everybody else on this planet you have basic human needs, yet do you ever stop and take stock of what you are getting out of life? How much love, importance, fun and security? Ask yourself and listen to your answers. If you don't do something to change this state of affairs it will stay exactly as it is. It is up to you.

Your personality and your life style are all determined by habit and – just like any other habit, nail-biting, rapping fingers on the table, or addictions like drinking and smoking – you can give them up. Anything can be changed if you want to enough.

Think for a moment about your own personality traits and habits and add them to your notebook. Are you lazy, talkative, energetic, quiet, fanatically tidy, inert? Do you usually wear bright clothes or drab ones? Do you spend a great deal of time in bed or are you up with the lark? Think about the way you speak to your friends and relations and the way others treat you; the way you behave at work and the way your colleagues treat you; the way you deal with shopkeepers, salesmen, repairmen. Then ask yourself if there is something about your personal style you'd like to change? Try changing a few small things at first so you don't feel too uncomfortable.

Change is rarely easy especially if these changes affect behaviour which has become natural to you over the years. But, if you received very strict messages in your childhood you may retain them until long after they are useful. My mum's favourites were 'Never go to bed and leave a sink full of washing-up'; 'Never put shoes on the table' and 'Never peep out of the net curtains to see who is at the door'. This, I was told, was very rude. I never really questioned why. The oh-so-common washing-up rule was probably born of a time when families were large and to leave all the dishes in the sink would have made things pretty awkward at breakfast time - when many people were up and about at five or six in the morning! The shoes she could only put down to a superstition about 'bad luck'. But I know now that Mum forbade me to peep out of the window in case the rent man was at the door and she had no money. If he saw me he would have known she was at home and she would have had to face an embarrassing situation. Do you know, I taught my children not to peep too and it wasn't until they questioned it that I even gave it a second thought.

A secure child is one who discovers that most of the information gleaned from his parents turns out to be true.

- It really does feel much nicer to wear dry trousers.
- It does feel warmer if I wear my mittens.
- If I touch the hot saucepan it really does hurt.

Some confusing data is bound to be picked up, so no matter how good a parent you try to be sometimes you will get it wrong - nobody is perfect. Children must find that out for themselves and eventually they do.

My daughter managed to open the garden gate and escape one day. I was fraught with worry. I scoured the whole neighbourhood knocking on the door of everyone we even vaguely knew in case she was there. Eventually, when I was returning home tearfully to ring the police, I saw her little red wellies on my neighbour's doorstep.

I hauled her out, shook her and shouted at her for wandering off without telling me. I often wonder what was her response. Fear, anger, frustration, bewilderment. She couldn't possibly have realized how worried I had been. My reaction was due to *my* distress.

The mature part of our subconscious (the Adult) is being

updated all the time. We cannot wipe out the memories we have already stored but we can stop them from playing such an important role in our life. When we receive a shock it revives feelings experienced as a child. The spontaneous, childlike part of an individual's personality (the Child) can react in the same way it did when that person was small and helpless.

This may stop that person from dealing with new situations. It may hold him or her back in many other ways. Many of our reactions are automatic and to become aware of them for the first time can be quite hard work.

Like a garden your problems need to be tended if they are not to become tangled and unmanageable. Planning is needed for what lies ahead. Regular maintenance will keep it in good working order so that healthy blooms appear later on.

SAYING NO

In large letters in your journal write: NO.

For many of us, saying no is the hardest thing we have to do. Employers, colleagues, friends and family, the homeless and a legion of flag-sellers and collectors for charity all weigh in with requests for money or time. Saying no is necessary if we are ever to have time, money and peace of mind. We have to refuse demands that steal our time and our choices. Saying no is everyone's privilege.

What about learning to say no to someone for the first time? Say NO loudly to yourself a few times. How does it sound? Strange? Different, certainly. When you have begun to feel a little more comfortable with it, I want you to try to take on the world at large. Remember you always have the right to say no, no matter how you choose to say it. You have the right to protect your own interests. Give youself a goal. Coerce yourself into saying no at least three times during the next week and put a tick in your journal whenever you do. The world won't fall apart. The person you say no to won't attack you. You can be as polite about it as you like, but say it. You are seldom obliged to explain. Saying no need not be rude. Done in the right way, it shows consideration for others – and yourself.

Once you get used to it you will never look back.
Practise some of these strategies:

- 'Let me have some time to think about it.'
- 'I'd love to do that for you but I can't say yes right now. Give me some time to see if I can work something out.'
  (Rarely do you have to say yes on the spot. This statement gives you time to come up with an excuse – if necessary – but the exercise is not for you to justify yourself by saying no. It is the means of being in control and making decisions for yourself.)
- 'I'm flattered that you have asked me. I would love to help but I'm just too busy to accept right now.'
- 'That's a very thoughtful offer, but I'm not in the position to take advantage of it at the moment.'
- 'I'm sorry you have this problem but I'm afraid it's just not possible for us to help this time.'
- 'We love your dinner parties, but I'm afraid we can't make it on that particular day.'

And to a collector when you have refused to contribute something and you are asked pointedly why, you could try smiling and saying, 'Because I'm mean.' Being humorous is a skilful way of saying no. Children and youngsters in particular respond to this one.

CHANGE

It is not easy to change old habits. In a way you have to pretend you are someone else. You must stop dreaming of that win on the pools, the magic windfall or romantic millionaire to help you along the way – you will be waiting for those things for ever. Instead take a pride in yourself and your skills and avoid the 'addiction to self-insults'. If you act as though you are worthwhile – even if you haven't started believing it yet – you will begin to see changes in the way others see you and ultimately you will notice they will treat you differently too. Your confidence will rise and you will have begun that upward spiral to success.

People spend much of their time dwelling on past events and dreaming about what might happen in the future – pipe dreams like winning the pools – falling in love with a millionaire – being famous – may take your mind off what is going on now but they don't bring you any closer to your goal. Non-assertive people criticize themselves whenever they get the chance. They remember their mistakes and forget their successes. They resent those who are successful and begrudge the achievements of those who didn't sit around waiting for Lady Luck to help them on their way – those who got on and did something with their lives.

Keep reminding yourself that your prime goal is to begin to love yourself and have compassion for yourself despite your faults. You will start satisfying your own needs without feeling guilty and praise yourself for trying – even if you don't succeed. And constantly ask yourself 'What do I need?' and 'What is right for me?'

It is incredibly exciting to discover that by your own thoughts and actions you can start building the sort of life you have wanted for yourself for so long. But before you can even begin to make even the smallest changes you must first accept that you are largely responsible for what happens to you and to believe that if circumstances are to change it is you and you alone that can bring about that change.

CHAPTER 8

Some Historical Background

The notion of getting in touch with negative influences in your life and taking charge of your inner self has been developed and expanded in different ways by countless psychiatrists since Freud began his work at the beginning of the century.

The Greeks were the first to write about psychology. Even the pre-Christians used folk psychology, using symbols and inducing trances in their attempts to find answers to their difficult problems in life.

Freud in the early 1900s was trained as a neurologist, and used analysis to find the origins of psychological problems. His extensive work suggested that warring factions existed in our unconscious. He gave names to these warring factions; the Superego (the restrictive controlling force), the Id (which provides instinctual drives), and the Ego (which acts as a kind of referee). And his theories led to the many and varied psychological schools of thought of today. However, he applied most of his genius to discovering how the mind works and the part that sexuality and aggression play in the development of human beings. He spent little time concentrating on how we might change things.

Now, developed from Freud's findings, there are many different schools of counselling. The main ones are:

HYPNOSIS

The hypnotic school of counselling was started by Franz Anton Mesmer (1734-1815). He regarded the processs of hypnotism as one that transports the client into another 'state of mind'. The hypnotic state is usually not quite as dramatic as demonstrations by showmen on the stage or television suggest. Hypnosis is a sleep-like state. Normal planning functions are reduced and the hypnotized person waits quietly for instructions from the hypnotist. The hypnotized person hears only one voice and blocks out all others. He or she can become completely immersed in a suggested role.

Post-hypnotic suggestion can also be used to encourage people to change certain behaviour patterns and give up addictions like drinking, nail-biting and smoking. It is often successful.

ANALYTIC COUNSELLING

The Analytic School of Counselling was started by Carl Gustav Jung (1875-1961), who, like Sigmund Freud, was a doctor of medicine. He wrote broadly on such complex topics as word association, mythology, religion, telepathy, spiritualism, dreams and even flying saucers, but he focused primarily on what he called the 'inherited collective unconscious'. This was Jung's term for that aspect of the unconscious shared by everyone, which has universal ideas or images and archetypes. He believed that several of these images evolved sufficiently to be treated as distinct systems. He turned to the whole field of mythology (which, he maintained, crossed all cultures) to explore the part that archetypal images play in the life of each human being. His therapy is concerned with a profound interpretation of these symbols and makes extensive use of them in dream analysis. Jung's point of view has been clearly summarized by E. A. Bennet in his book *What Jung Really Said* (1966), and by Robin Robertson in *Beginner's Guide to Jungian Psychology*.

HUMANISTIC COUNSELLING

The Humanistic School of Counselling is largely the creation of Abraham Maslow, who had his own distinctive views. He projected another, equally important, set of values into modern psychology. He suggested that psychology was too concerned either with that which was neurotic and disturbed or with that which was explainable. Maslow developed a science based on self-development, knowledge and understanding, client-centred and non-directive. Carl Rogers (1902–1987) was the first person to use the term 'counselling'. He and Alfred Adler (1870–1937) are also associated with the humanistic approach.

BEHAVIOURIST COUNSELLING

The Behaviourist School of Counselling is a term used to cover several behaviour therapies which share the assumption that neurotic behaviours (like obsessional or compulsive traits) and difficulties with learning can be objectively treated, independently from the rest of a person's personality. This type of therapy was initiated by B. F. Skinner. His approach is concerned with the effects that certain behaviour patterns have on our environment. He believed that people could be conditioned into being happy. Most modern psychologists agree that the way people behave and what they actually do is what really matters. Behaviour Therapy is basically a learning therapy. It assumes that symptoms are due to maladaptive behaviours and conditioning and aims to teach people to change their own reactions. It is used frequently to cure phobias and other behavioural disorders where it is possible to isolate the symptoms from 'normal' behaviour.

During the 1950s many more schools of psychology were evolved. Their approaches were geared towards helping people get in touch with their inner thoughts and helping them to move forward and make changes. Gregory Bateson and others looked in detail at the nature of the interaction of individuals one with another. Their insights led to the development of schools of thought used nowadays by many types of therapist.

These therapies encompass different theories, and therapists and counsellors help people overcome psychological problems with this mix and match approach.

More recently Dr Eric Berne (whose career began in the 1950s) developed the concept of Transactional Analysis. This is a simple tool for making changes to your life. He explains his theories in words that anyone can understand. He identifies what often lies behind our negative behaviour and teaches us how to move forward. It is a learning device which aims to help calm the inner fears that impede you. Learning to control your inner voice helps you to grow and move away from past events which are cluttering minds and affecting behaviour.

We have seen that different messages are picked up from different people around us and we try to make sense of them. It is important to remember as we grow, teachers, friends, parents, neighbours, family, church leaders, the police, and the media all add to our store of messages. It is suggested that messages like these stay in our subconscious and are played back to us time and time again.

- 'Don't eat with your mouth open.'
- 'Don't point.'
- 'Cleanliness is next to Godliness.'
- 'Big boys don't cry.'
- 'If you don't work hard, you won't get on in life.'
- 'The meek shall inherit the earth.'
- 'Honesty is the best policy.'
- 'Manners maketh man.'
- 'If you can't say something nice don't say anything at all.'
- 'Sit like a lady.'
- 'Don't cry – you're a man.'
- 'Why can't you be like your brother?'

I'm sure you can find hundreds more that you recognize. Berne suggests that everyone hears unspoken messages like this playing in their minds. We translate them into things we should, must or ought to do or should, must or ought not to do.

To help us understand what is going on in our subconscious mind, Berne suggests we each have three subpersonalities, the Parent, the Adult and the Child. The Parent is the subpersonality who, as well as being the inner voice that supports and nourishes us, is the one who initiates our self-criticism. The Parent records messages like 'It's rude to interrupt', 'Boys don't cry' and 'Ladies don't sit like that'.

The Child is the subpersonality which is delightfully spontaneous but it is also the part of us that stamps the foot, is disobedient, and at times, insolent. The Child responds openly, impulsively and naturally and is dominated by feelings. The Child within us stays throughout our life. The Child constantly seeks to please, to be good and to gain approval but is also quite rebellious, 'I shan't, so there!' The Child is irritating and annoying, he tempts us to break rules, encourages us to run with the wind in our hair, is lighthearted, and full of fun. It is our Child that produces sulks, but who allows us to cry for other people's hurts and sentimental books and films. The records that the Child plays in our heads are 'Why me?' and 'It's not fair' and it is the Child within us that feels the hurt when others don't respond to our moods.

The Adult, on the other hand, is the wise, realistic and well-adjusted side of our personality. The Adult part of our make-up described by Berne is the sensible, rational part of our mind. He is also logical, grown up, and responsible. He endures pain and makes plans for the future. He is made up of parents, authority figures and guardians of our childhood. The emotions associated with this part of ourselves are much more appropriate to the situations we are in now. Berne says that your brain is like a computer. You feed in the information and it comes out with the correct answer. This does not mean that the Adult part of our brain has no emotion but that the emotions are more appropriate. All the reactions of your Adult are based on experiences that happened during those important early years. Berne suggests that we can work out what is happening inside us in terms of how these three important parts or subpersonalities interact with each other.

Using Berne's theory we can begin to filter out some of our

feelings and understand our own and others' reactions. I will go into his theory a little deeper.

Berne supposes that as young children we learn most things from the adults around us quite naturally. These adults are any people in our young life who take on the parental role. They can be step-parents, foster parents, kindergarten teachers, house masters, grandparents, aunts and uncles, in fact anyone who has played a significant part in bringing us up. Childhood experiences add shape and colour to our lives and they help form our personalities; personalities which are built from a tangle of dreams, hopes and plans for the future which we have picked up from messages received right back to the first moments of our lives. Facial expressions, cuddles and soothing words are all registered and defined in their own way. Later on, words of love, delight, tenderness, but anger and disapproval too, are added to this knowledge. Most of our childhood experiences are healthy ones but sometimes as a mature person the Child in us takes over. This Child can strongly influence the Adult and we may lose much of our confidence. Even though the Adult is fairly sure of what action to take in a situation, the Child inside may undermine us and we may feel very uncomfortable. Inner battles go on and we become unsure of ourselves. We find decision-making difficult. We are often not aware of what is happening. Our energy is sapped, leaving us feeling miserable and confused.

Susan's husband had been discovered in bed with her cousin. Susan had always seen herself as understanding and forgiving. She had guided many friends through similar experiences, always encouraging them to talk things through with their partners and to forgive and forget. But now it was her turn. When David admitted what he'd done she felt such powerful emotion rise up inside her that her head started to swim and she quickly lost control of her feelings. She felt sick and giddy. No matter how much she tried to convince herself that he really was sorry and that he meant every word of his promise never to do such a thing again, still the feelings were there. She couldn't eat, she lost weight. She went to stay with her sister for a while who, against her parents' wishes, talked Susan into giving David another chance. Her sister helped her to decide that she wanted to work things out. She did still love him. She tried but she was still tormented by the anger and jealousy. Visions of the infidelity kept flooding her mind. She became depressed. She felt as though her heart was breaking and she thought that no matter how hard she tried she would never be able to forgive him. She told herself that it was inevitable that she would drive him away for good.

The Parent within her was playing some recordings from her childhood:

- 'What will people think if you stay with him after what he did?'
- 'Everyone will think you are weak if you don't teach him a lesson.'
- 'He couldn't possibly love you if he slept with someone else.'

The Child was saying:

- 'It's not fair – my cousin always took everything of mine.'
- 'I'll sulk and make myself ill – that'll teach him.'
- 'If I run away he'll be sorry' or
- 'What did I do to stop him loving me?'
- 'If I'm horrible to David he'll leave me and then I'll be lonely.'

The Child felt unloved and as these feelings surfaced, Susan sobbed and sobbed. Then at last she took a deep breath and tried to take control.

After the tears and many angry words, shouting and uncontrolled emotion the Adult inside Susan was able to surface. She could step back from the situation which for so long had seemed hopeless. She began to see the problem as a challenge. She told David of the battle that was going on within her and said she felt they needed professional help from a counsellor to help them work through their difficulties. David too was going through his own set of feelings of guilt and self-blame.

But with help from a counsellor they were able to resolve their conflict and work towards a shared future.

For Berne's Transactional Analysis to sort out a problem, all three sides of the personality must get together on an equal and mutually respecting level. Thomas A. Harris in his popular book *I'm OK you're OK*, published by Pan, talks about this theory in further detail. It is well worth reading.

DR WILDER PENFIELD

The 1950s were important years in the field of psychotherapy. At that time the famous neurosurgeon Dr Wilder Penfield, from McGill University in Montreal, made a very important breakthrough and discovery about the workings of the brain whilst treating sufferers of epilepsy. He discovered that when certain parts of the brain were stimulated with probes, past events and the feelings that were associated with them were remembered in detail. Penfield also claimed that an event and its associated feelings are inextricably bound together in the brain so that one cannot be evoked without the other. When memories were relived, the emotions bound with them felt as intense as if they had just happened.

The actual process of storing this seemingly pointless information is chemical and not fully understood – even by specialists – but one thing is clear; the feelings associated with a particular memory stay around even after the actual memory fades. These stored feelings affect the way we react to certain situations. A hug may make you feel good because it revives memories of hugs which you enjoyed long ago. However, if hugs revive less happy feelings, the contrary may be the case. Then, getting close to someone may be difficult.

Music, smells, sights and sounds can all evoke poignant memories and their associated feelings, decades after the events. Have you ever been overwhelmed by sadness or been cheered up on hearing a particular piece of music? Or maybe it's the smell of a certain flower, the sound of an aeroplane in the distance, or is it the glimpse of a familiar face that prompts your most emotional response? Somewhere, buried in your memory, there are sure to be poignant, sad, happy and other emotional reactions triggered by one of these sensual experiences.

Kathleen lost her mother when she was a small child. At family parties her mum would don a top hat and carry her grandfather's silver-topped cane as she strode up and down the room singing her version of the popular World War II song 'The Lambeth Walk'. Kathleen was devastated by the death of her mum. So it was not surprising to find that whenever that tune was played she was engulfed in powerful feelings of sadness. I met her years later when she had finally started working through her grief. She did manage, eventually, to listen to 'Mum's song' without being reduced to floods of tears, but it still evoked some sadness.

GEORGE R. BACH

In my search for different ways of looking at internal human conflicts I came across some enlightening books by the author George R. Bach. He describes our inner battles as being acted out by a series of demons which he blames for the confusion and turmoil that goes on in our minds. In his books *You're Driving Me Crazy* and *The Inner Enemy* he explains how 'deep-seated discontent expresses itself in destructive ways in the context of intimate relationships' and he describes his methods for dealing with these inner demons to help people maintain a balance between their positive and negative voices.

Bach's words seem to have brought together for me all the different theories and techniques for making changes. In order to make changes that will enrich our life by improving assertiveness and confidence, I like to imagine, as he did, that in all of us there is some kind of 'personal gremlin' made up of all the creatures of our unconscious, and who makes us resist change for the better.

If we are to make changes in the way we live our life we must get to know this little chap better. We have to learn to make him behave better and we must stand up to him.

Bach's little gremlin is formed by all our past hurts and he seems to encapsulate Berne's Parent/Adult/Child, Freud's Ego/

Superego/Id, Jung's Collective Unconscious and all the messages and records that are inside our minds. He is the little fellow who can be blamed for your unassertive traits. He's the one always throwing spanners in your works, the imp who makes you feel as if there is a limit to how much you can learn to do or achieve. He's the one who helps make things go wrong. He tempts you to eat too much (or diet because you imagine you are too fat). He teases you with cigarettes so you smoke too many, or takes away your resistance to other addictive substances like alcohol or the humble caffeine and he can make you feel dreadfully guilty about it afterwards.

You can tune in to this inner voice (however you like to imagine him) and get to know and understand him. You can stand up to him and reason with him and eventually you will begin to win some of the battles in your progress towards the positive. You will start to take charge of your life.

Bach asks you to imagine that your gremlin coerces, or restricts you as you 'internalize' all the data you stored, starting from the cradle onwards. Much of what he tells you is actually geared to protecting you from harm (actual or perceived). For instance, he stops you playing with sharp instruments and fire, and from walking close to the edge of precipices. He stops you from walking on thin ice and from talking to strangers. The trouble is that some of these messages become confused. Often they are inconsistent. The adults around you as you are growing up - who help you to develop your inner voice - may tell you to do one thing while they do another. They explain how important it is to tell the truth and then ask you to tell the insurance man they aren't in. They tell you it's bad to smoke while reaching for their fortieth fag of the day. And with a cupboard full of brandy and whisky they tell you how drink can destroy your life. If the recordings get too confusing - and they do - the Child within us has to make some sense out of it all. Small wonder he sometimes gets it wrong.

In some cases children come from violent or deprived environments. There, many conflicting messages are picked up, and the results can be disturbing. If, for example, a parent beats the child because he dares to experiment with new skills, the child may block out messages his parent gives him altogether and become negative and withdrawn. But if the messages which are picked up are clear and harmonious they can be heard playing throughout life. They are a strong, positive influence. Maybe like Bach you can imagine that your gremlin is using all this data to test you out. It may help you as you journey into self-discovery.

The internal arguments have been described in many ways. Some see them as conflict between good and evil, some as our lower and higher natures and some as our inner and outer selves. One thing is for sure, we are all extremely complicated characters with many facets. Some see the positive side of themselves as justice, others as wisdom and most of us see it as love. But it is true for us all that our positive side is constantly battling with the negative and that that negative side in its many guises is what I imagine (as Bach did) to be that little gremlin.

Before you can even attempt to place your foot on the first rung of the assertiveness ladder, you must try as we have seen to tune in to this inner voice. Get to know and understand your own argumentative little gremlin who spoils almost everything you do. Tell him where to get off. Stand up to him, reason with him, and eventually you will begin to win some of the arguments.

You can live without feeling habitual guilt. You can do the things you dreamed about doing while gazing out of the steamy kitchen window, or staring blankly at your computer, but never imagined you would really do. Let go and be childlike and uninhibited for a change. Be happy.

Talk to friends about their inner voices. You will find similarities and differences that will surprise you. Some of these voices will have been holding you back ever since you can remember. Do some detective work and start writing down your findings in your journal. Look at it every day and see what your inner voice has been telling you. Don't make the changes straight away, just listen and watch what is going on. Try to work out why you didn't face some particular challenge. Ask yourself what part of your subconscious told you that you were not capable, or that the job was too difficult, or not for you. Remember your little gremlin is very clever. He will justify his reasons for holding you back by saying he doesn't want to see you hurt or embarrassed or ridiculed - and if you keep listening to him and believing what he says you will stay in your rut. But if you start telling your gremlin to stop poking his nose in your business, and start taking a few risks (tiny ones at first) like changing your hairstyle, the way you dress or by trying an exotic meal - you'll see it's not half as risky as it might seem.

CHAPTER 9

Communication and Body Language

Getting to know another person and sharing intimacy at any level involves talking and listening to each other, and becoming sensitive to the other's needs. This cocktail of basic skills combined with body language and a little intuition form the art of communication. For some this comes naturally and yet for many the ability to communicate remains one of the most difficult skills to acquire. It is a subtle art which grows out of everyday experiences, yet many never grasp it. However, these skills, like any others, can be learned.

To be a good communicator you must also be a good listener. There's more to listening than just allowing words to waft round your ears. To listen well you must concentrate, evaluate and understand whatever it is the other person is telling you. It means reading between the lines. A good listener really tries to understand what the other is saying and then lets him or her know that he understands. He makes his interest apparent by using a subtle amount of eye contact and by giving the speaker his complete attention.

Communication determines the quality of our relationships with those with whom we come in contact. And if one element is missing from the cocktail it can be very easy to pick up misleading messages. For instance you are in Spain and your car is stopped by a police officer. With a raised voice he launches into what sounds like a reprimand and you have little knowledge of the language. Are you scared? Probably! Your mind would be racing. 'How do I get out of this?' Visions of yourself locked in a Spanish prison flash before you. You ask yourself 'What on earth did I do wrong?' 'What can I say?'

You decide to show the policeman your passport and in a feeble attempt at Spanish (which in the panic seems to have deserted you entirely) you say you don't understand. The police officer looks at your passport and smiles. He says in perfect English that his wife is British, she comes from London. You take a deep breath – a sigh of relief. You ask the police officer why he stopped you and he tells you the road has been closed farther on due to rock falls and he's advising everyone to turn left at the next junction.

Communication is the key. From this example you can see that both non-verbal and verbal communication determines our relationships. Being able to communicate what you want, feel or need to those you meet is desirable of course, but it is not enough on its own. Empathy, respect and sensitivity are also characteristics without which an assertive person would become a bull in a china shop charging through the ideas, feelings and opinions of others. However, properly learned, sensitively taught assertive techniques can help forge the way towards much more fulfilling lives.

Communicating assertively also means having empathy with the person with whom you are conversing. Empathy is putting yourself in someone else's place and trying to see the world through their eyes. A conversation is a medley of observation, empathy, listening and respect. Never assume that everything you know or believe is absolutely true. All our opinions are coloured by preferences, assumptions and conditioning. Every person has the right to his point of view (even if you disagree with it) and should never be put down, or made to feel ridiculous. An assertive person shows a desire to understand another person's point of view. Encouraging someone to explore his or her own ideas is important if you are to open up friendly communications. Forcing your opinions upon others is arrogant and sometimes aggressive. It is NOT being assertive. You will find that by allowing others the space to share their ideas and opinions with you, you will benefit in the long run and they will be more prepared to give you the space to talk about your own thoughts.

It can be quite daunting to be in company with others who share an expertise which you don't. It's understandable. They may be computer experts, medics or car mechanics. It doesn't matter what their field is. All that matters to you at the time is that they are talking 'above your head'. You feel stupid, as though you were invisible. At work this is most apparent between the boss and the employees. The boss is interested in running the business, in plans for future development and in taking the chair at meetings. The employees are more interested in the job in hand: working out new computer programmes, faster ways of removing wheel hubs, or how to get the ward tidy before Sister comes back on duty. They are concerned with the practicalities. Communication here is of prime importance, so don't allow feelings of inadequacy to arise. Remind yourself that even a most experienced and intelligent person can feel like a fish out of water in a new situation.

Non-assertive people are often at their most terrified when they have to open a conversation. They begin sentences with 'er', 'um', 'I'm sorry', 'Excuse me', 'I'm sorry to bother you', 'Would you mind if'. Does this sound familiar? People often expect others to guess what they are feeling and to read their minds. How often have you been angry, upset or frustrated because someone couldn't understand what was wrong. They didn't appreciate that you were tired, ill or busy. They didn't know you were already overworked or that you were doing something important. They couldn't tell you were just drained or disinterested in the work in hand. Of course they didn't know. You hadn't told them and they are not psychic!

Of course body language, which I'll discuss later, does give out some clues but they are often misread or even overlooked. Time after time you may be misunderstood, misinterpreted, mistreated until finally boof! you blow your top – usually over something trivial – and you leave people open-mouthed and bewildered by behaviour which is totally out of character.

Words are just another way of communication which we use in conjunction with all the other symbolic and non-verbal means, which, consciously or unconsciously, we have acquired over the years. Effective communication is simply the organization of these to be clearly understood. Communication has only been effective when your listener knows exactly what you mean.

It is easy for the two mechanics, the two computer buffs, or the two nurses I mentioned earlier, to understand each other because they use the same technical terminology. Specialized non-verbal language and signals is part of your life. Think about how you might feel speaking to your insurance agent, your solicitor, your doctor. You may need to have things clarified several times before you fully understand their meaning. But it is vital if you are to become a good communicator. If you are shy, scared and have a low self-esteem, of course it is going to be more difficult. But it is not impossible.

Common language and common experience are not the only components of good communication.

In Britain we often use the state of the weather to break the ice with another person. In a more formal setting, an interviewer will not immediately ask an inteviewee a complicated question. He will usually open with a bland question or two about the interviewee's life and previous experience before launching into the more relevant nitty-gritty. In every situation we need to find some common ground to launch into good communication.

So start from the simplest, non-controversial openings, let's say in the dentist's waiting room. 'It's hot in here, isn't it?' This gives the other person the chance to let you know whether they want to converse with you. A simple 'yes' with averted eyes will let you know either that they don't want to talk or that they are shyer than you are. But a reply 'Yes, this room is always hot. I think the thermostat is broken.' – and you are in. You have made contact and established a new relationship, albeit in its infancy. You might try an open-ended question next, like 'What are you here for?' and again the reply will give a clue to whether they want to enlarge on the topic or whether they would rather read the magazines scattered on the table. Sometimes people are reluctant to talk about anything more than general issues like the weather, others give you their life history without much prompting. But a good conversation opener gives the person the option to talk or not, as they wish. You have asked for tacit permission to step inside that person's boundaries.

But sadly it is not quite as easy as it might sound. Not everything is as cut and dried. Your own language spoken in an alien way can give a false impression or make seemingly false statements. Accents or colloquial expressions, too, can give out confusing messages. We may make judgements about people which are quite wrong. In this country we work at giving these impressions by having elocution lessons, by raising or lowering our tone of voice and even dressing for effect. Some companies have separate dining rooms for managers and workpeople. This gives out the message that managers are better or higher up in the pecking order. Different modes of dress may be used as props to the body language which emphasizes certain messages. Managers wear suits and sit behind impressive desks to give themselves an air of authority.

BODY LANGUAGE

Body language is an important part of the multifaceted art of communication and one which is not always immediately understood. It is the term used for an intricate system which communicates information about feelings and emotions through non-verbal channels. It involves gestures, body positions, facial expressions and other non-verbal signs. These can either help or hinder your first impressions. From head to toe messages are given off which form a language – a body language of love, of hate and of every other emotion in between. For a million years, before spoken language began, body language was the only form of communication.

Clothes can certainly make statements about their wearers and how they see themselves. Postures and gestures too. Hands pushed deep into pockets may help someone appear to be standing firm in a debate. A person may clench his knuckles to show aggression, anger or fear and they may grip their lapels to demonstrate arrogance or pride.

Arms folded across the chest can be seen as a defence – a sign of self-comfort – or they may signal a certain wariness. Watch how some people automatically cross their body with their arms when someone says something they do not understand or which they find offensive. Resting the arms behind the back and so baring the chest can be a signal of confidence. Standing with hands on hips or fingers tucked in a belt or pocket as if in a gun holster can show aggression or sexuality. Displaying an open wrist can tell someone blatantly that you are interested in them sexually.

Feet too can be real giveaways! You can tell from looking at feet if the person is angry or frustrated. They may stamp or kick out at a chair or some imaginary object, or they can be used tenderly in sex play under the table. They can be elevated to the desk top to show that the person owns or would like to own this territory. And those same feet can be 'under the table', stretched out in rather too relaxed an attitude in someone else's house. You can show interest by pointing your feet towards the person you are attracted to or you can exclude them by turning them away.

If you want to make headway when walking through a crowd always look in the direction you are going. If you don't, you will collide with people coming the other way. Next time you are in a crowd concentrate on looking ahead and you will glide through without mishap. If you gaze around idly as you walk, people will bump into you continually. Pedestrians notice where others are looking and in which direction they are going without being aware of it. To be positive in gait and focus can save a great deal of time when rushing along a crowded pavement.

Some men and women can walk into a room, quickly make a choice of the romantically available partners in the room and, almost as if by magic, find themselves in conversation with them. They seem to have built-in sensors which pick up these alluring waves. Research into animal courtship reveals that animals use a series of courtship gestures to make their instincts known. Human beings also send out these non-verbal signals. Some people are acutely aware of these courtship gestures, others are totally blind to them and although many of these gestures are quite unconscious, some are quite deliberate. The best place to observe these signals is by a swimming pool or on the beach. Have you noticed that when two 'interested' people of the opposite sex approach each other their stomachs are pulled in, they become more aware of their posture, their way of walking and the way they hold their heads? They pass – smile (or not) – and their posture returns to normal.

In an urban situation a man may straighten his tie, brush imaginary dust from his coat or fiddle with his shirt cuff. A woman may touch her hair, place her hands on her hips, make eye contact and you can usually assume there is a suggestion of sexuality in the air if a couple talk with their hips, feet and body facing one another. Sexual excitement causes pupils to dilate and a slight flush to appear on the face and neck. For years blusher has been used by women to imitate this flushing effect and make her appear sexually excited or aroused.

Exposure of the palms of the hands can also be tantalizing. So can the intimate look that holds another's gaze for a split second longer than normal. A man may stand with his shoulders back and his hands resting in his belt or in his pockets to emphasize his size. His downward pointing thumbs emphasize the genital area. To light a fire in the man she desires, a woman may coyly tilt her head, lower her eyelids then hold a man's gaze for a second before turning away.

Lowering the body and putting the head on one side can signal deference. It is a means of establishing positions within a relationship. Those who feel inferior constantly sink down within themselves and appear subservient. The more humble a person feels the lower he stoops his body. And unfair though it seems, tall people do command more authority, particularly if they stand up straight. Gone are the days when a tall woman felt obliged to stoop to disguise her height. Happily, those inches are, usually, a matter of pride today.

If a person stands with shoulders drooped, walks with a heavy step, and with what looks like a heavy heart, we say 'they have the weight of the world on their shoulders'. That is probably just how they feel. Miserable feelings and constant worry can knock the stuffing out of you – dragging you down emotionally. This is apparent in an individual's posture.

Tension, too, shows itself. A person under stress may look stiff and awkward, he may lift his shoulders, tense his neck muscles and have difficulty in turning his head. For people like this, learning to relax the body can also help relax the mind. Relaxation techniques are a must if you are emotionally drained or tense.

But despite all this complicated body-talk the future is not all doom and gloom. There is a lot you can do to make your life happier, more rewarding and more exciting. It just takes care and thought along with some practice.

If you watch carefully you will notice that body language can actually contradict verbal communication. A simple example of this might be when somebody is saying 'Of course I love you' whilst shaking their head from side to side in unconscious denial. It can include movement of a part or all of the body to communicate an emotional message to the world.

In addition to sending messages it can be used to relax and disarm others – a light touch on an arm together with a reassuring look can say 'trust me'. The brush of someone's hand or an arm around someone's shoulder can convey quite direct messages but these touches must be applied at the right moment and in the right context or they can be completely misconstrued. We pick up these ways of communicating unconsciously. Some of us get it right, some do not. Unnecessary touching can sometimes be quite inappropriate, and cause stressful reactions in the other person – as many young men quickly find out. Touching a girl at the wrong moment will quickly turn her off!

We are all sending out non-verbal messages. We say 'don't talk to me – I want to be alone with my thoughts'. We say 'welcome' or 'don't touch'. Some of these messages we act out unconsciously - others are quite deliberate. We screw up our noses when we are puzzled; we raise our eyebrows when we are surprised. We cross our arms and legs to protect ourselves. We tap our fingers with impatience, place a finger to our temple when we are thinking and shrug our shoulders to say 'It's immaterial to me' or 'I don't care'. Some body language applies only to one culture. Other responses like smiling, frowning, and raising eyebrows, cross all cultural barriers. We can all show hate, fear, amusement, joy and sadness without consciously learning how.

The most obvious sign that someone has a low self-esteem or is lacking in confidence is seen in the simple act of shaking hands. Very rarely will you come across someone with a weak handshake who has a lot of social confidence. Nor would a confident individual look away while being introduced. Assertive people enter a conversation with feelings of curiosity and pleasure, wondering if their new acquaintance will interest them or become a friend.

In the workplace too a knowledge of body language can be most useful. Posture can be a good indicator of attitude and status. However, I must emphasize that all body language study can only give an indication of what might be going on. Don't make assumptions when trying to pick up pointers; only use these clues alongside other means of communication to build up an overall picture of a person or a situation.

PERMITTED SPACE

We all have a certain air space around our bodies that we claim unconsciously as our personal or permitted space. This space is different in different cultures, and depends on the density of the population in the place where a person was reared. It is culturally determined. In Western cultures the air space we need in our most personal permitted space is usually 6-18 inches for people to whom we are emotionally close - parents, lovers, children, spouses and close friends and relatives.

The permitted space which we tolerate at business lunches,

cocktail parties, and social or friendly gatherings is between 18–48 inches and the distance we keep from strangers like the repairman, the postman or local shopkeeper or people we do not know very well can be between 4 and 12 feet. The distance at which we choose to stand when we are speaking publicly is rarely closer than 12 feet.

To move inside someone's personal zone too soon is to risk offence. If you want people to feel comfortable with you in these different situations you must 'keep your distance'. The closer you get to someone emotionally the closer you are allowed to get into their permitted space. The different intimate zone levels of different cultures can easily lead to misunderstandings. If a person from one culture gets too close and the other keeps backing away – both are endeavouring to maintain the space they find comfortable. It can be quite amusing to watch two people from different cultures moving around the room as one enters the other's permitted space and the other – feeling 'invaded' – backs away. So be aware if someone moves away from you. You may be wise not to move closer. Of course you may need to change your deodorant!

Eye contact is another finely balanced skill. It is increased if someone is interested in getting a message across. It is a good indication that someone is paying attention to what we are saying. If people are distracted or are averting their eyes when you are speaking you can bet your life they are not really listening and you might as well give up. We avert our eyes when we have lost interest in what someone is saying, if we don't particularly like the person who is talking or if what they are saying offends. Increased eye contact is usually a good indicator that you like the person or are interested in what he or she is saying.

In a group it is usually quite easy to detect who is the leader (whether official or not) as you will find other people are all trying to make eye contact with this person. So looking at people increases the impact of what we are saying and shows others that we are interested in them. However, be sure you don't overdo it. Don't get inside the other person's permitted space and don't stare. If you have difficulty in talking to people at work and would like to improve these skills try these strategies on people you meet as you go about your life; shopkeepers, people in queues or fellow travellers. Watch what happens if you stand too close, if you don't maintain eye contact or if you overdo it. Remember if you are to get it right – practise, practise, practise.

VIVE LA DIFFÉRENCE OR BRIDGING THE CONVERSATIONAL GAP!

Men and women are not only different in physical and biological makeup. They are worlds apart in the way they think and in the way they speak. The words we use to make conversation are affected by our expressions, gestures and movements. Our lives are a series of conversations. We try to make sense of what someone is trying to tell us, yet we are thwarted at every turn, not only by the other person's culture, background and class, but by their varying conversational styles, their age and most importantly, their sex. Yes, our relationships show that a man and a woman invariably interpret the same conversation in completely different ways.

Even if we form relationships with others of the same sex and work in an all-female or all-male environment there is still little chance of avoiding contact with people of the opposite sex altogether. So for all of us it is an area we are bound to face at some time.

There are gender differences in ways of speaking between men and women. We need to identify these differences and understand them if we are to make successful relationships with the opposite sex. One thing we should never do is accuse the opposite sex of being stupid, weird or just plain wrong if they see things differently. If we can begin to recognize and understand these differences we may then be able to take them into account and possibly find different and improved ways of communicating successfully. Only by understanding each other's styles and by taking the time to think about our own options can we begin to realize what opportunities can be explored. If we can avoid the misunderstandings we meet daily in our dealings with the opposite sex we will be in a better position to find a shared language in which to communicate. This is as important in the workplace and in all social situations as it is with your loved ones, your family and the ordinary people with whom you come in contact every day.

'You live on a different planet!'; 'Where on earth did you get that idea?'; 'That's not what I said at all!' - all these are familiar exchanges we hear every day. But although we do all live on the same planet, it very often appears that we are light years away from each other in understanding. Even people brought up in the same house with the same parents grow up with totally alien ways of communicating with each other.

Women have been brought up to think it is unfeminine to express themselves strongly. 'Men don't like pushy women'; 'A woman's place is in the home'; 'Women are passive - they are the givers and the carers'. Things are changing but often for every two steps women take forward, they take one back. As soon as problems arise they scurry back to the safety of their familiar role. For years women have felt put down and de-meaned by masculine ideology. However, slowly but surely they are gaining independence. Sadly, however, in certain environ-ments, they often have to work much harder than men to gain the same recognition. They have constantly to prove them-selves.

These differences are nurtured unconsciously by our parents, our relations and our peer groups. Boys and girls may be brought up together in the same country, the same village or even the same house but they will still evolve different ways of communicating. During early nursery or school days children spend much of their time playing with children of the same sex. Their preferred games are as different as their way of using language.

Young boys tend to collect in larger groups. They often have a leader who organizes them all. They gain status by telling exaggerated stories of their prowess and by challenging others. Later they gain recognition by telling jokes or exchanging stories of sexual conquests. Their groups have complex rules. They jockey for status by boasting and arguing about who is best at games or at attracting members of the opposite sex and they play games of dare. Young girls tend to choose one close pal who plays a central role in her life. Groups of girls are trusting and intimate. They usually play fairly noncompetitive games or those in which they all take turns. They play ball games and skipping and they join in the fun of making things like the tube of 'French knitting' made with a cotton reel with four nails, or sewing and knitting. Until recently they have been expected to be modest – never boastful – and they rarely give orders to each other. Although I have noticed a change towards more assertive behaviour apparent in even quite young girls, it is still true that they challenge each other less frequently and quiet moments are still spent sitting, chatting and sharing their dreams and plans. They are more concerned with being liked than being important.

As girls develop into women they continue to share secrets and ever more intimate conversations with each other. They tend to match troubles when sharing these intimacies. Rapport is reinforced by the implied message 'you are not alone'. They become closer when a problem is shared. When a woman attempts to do this in a conversation with a man, he will often take offence. He feels the woman is denying his experience and capping it with one of her own.

Men see themselves as problem-solvers and whilst women may accept help from a man on practical problems like repairing a leaky roof, women can resent it when males try to help them solve their emotional problems for them. They feel that emotional problems are their domain – they are the carers of this world. Men in turn feel resentful when their partner refuses to take their advice, which they interpret as reducing their status.

Because each conversational style is so different, it is inevitable that misunderstandings will arise. Learning about the differences isn't enough on its own to alter the way we talk to members of the opposite sex, but with increased understanding of other people's ways of using language we should get closer to being heard and being able to understand each other.

A man comes home from the office and flops into an armchair saying, 'I've had a frustrating day at work - everything seemed to go wrong. I even upset the boss over a complete misunderstanding.' The wife, trying to sympathize, replies, 'I know how you feel. My day has been a bit like that too. The kids have driven me up the wall and the lady in the corner shop thought I KNEW the baby had helped himself to some toffees.' Instead of making the husband feel better, he begins to feel angry. 'Why are you belittling my problems? You have no idea at all about what it's like having my sort of responsibility.' His wife replies, 'I'm not belittling your problems! I'm just trying to let you see I understand how you must be feeling.' His reply - 'Well you don't.' The result is that both people are now angry, misunderstood and the evening may be completely spoiled.

Today many important changes are taking place, but for the foreseeable future both men and women are going to continue to experience difficulties in all areas of life - from the workplace to the bedroom - because important changes like these evolve slowly. Women's expectations nowadays are higher at one level than they have ever been. At another level their programming - born of generations of subserviency - is still coming to the surface. Both women and men are bound to suffer from confusion as these internal battles continue. Women wonder if working towards this new-found independence is worth all the trouble it causes in their relationships. It is not surprising that some may wonder if they shouldn't have left things as they were, with women accepting the subservient, motherly role and leaving most of the decision-making to the men. And men are increasingly being left unsure of how they are expected to behave. In many cases intelligent, sensitive and hard-working men feel emasculated because their working wives are earning as much or more money than they are and seem to be able to juggle work, mothering, and home-care with comparative ease, whilst they are only just about getting to grips with the washing-up, and their pride takes another hammering.

Sheila is an independent career woman. She is esteemed by her peers in her career as a solicitor. Her opinions are highly valued and her staff treat her with the greatest respect. But at home things are very different. As soon as she walks through the door her programming, grown from her experiences, takes over. Her husband's wishes are paramount and override all her own. Lest she hurts him, she goes to great lengths to reassure him that his career is first and her own is second in her life. She gives in to her husband's choice of house decoration, his wishes regarding the children, what they eat, and where they go for their holidays. She is terrified of trampling on his fragile pride as he watches her career blossom. She feels embarrassed about her success. She feels that to be dominant in the home would disturb the status quo and put the relationship at risk.

Another common scenario is one in which a man fears he may lose his freedom and so backs off when a woman starts to show familiarity. The woman, who was just beginning to feel that she and her partner were becoming close, fears losing this growing intimacy. She attempts to close the gap that is growing between them by becoming more intimate. He becomes distant and behaves in a detached manner – pulling away from a woman with whom he had a potentially great relationship. Stresses begin to show, tensions rise, as each fears what the other may or may not be thinking. Before they know it, doubts begin which may cause the relationship to flounder, when with a little more understanding it might have grown into something wonderful. Understanding each other's ways of thinking and speaking is a step towards breaking this destructive spiral.

Men and women communicate affection for one another in different ways too. In the most intimate of moments they behave in ways specific to their gender. When a woman and a man lie down together in bed, or on a rug in a leafy glade you can be sure the man will lie on his back while the woman curls up beside him with her body curved and nestled against his. She will rest her head on his chest or on his shoulder and his arm may be placed around her as though to protect her or lovingly stroke her hair. These gender-specific positions are repeated automatically in daily situations. They feel comfortable – absolutely right. We are constantly reassured by the sight of similar groupings on television, big-screen films and in countless other situations. We are symbolically underpinning the imbalanced relationship of man seen as solid, firm, dependable, and woman as weak and in need of protection. This example is just one of a multitude of gender asymmetries that strengthen status difference between the sexes.

These asymmetries are often seen as quite natural reminders that male domination in many areas is very special and very important. They can be carried into many intimate moments without causing problems. However, notions of what is regarded as 'naturally' male or female are beginning to change and it is not surprising therefore that there is some misunderstanding when men behave towards women as loving protectors. They imply that their role is deserving of special respect, just as though the women were helpless children and so naturally subordinate. But the 'privilege' of protection brings with it the loss of rights for women, and the implication that they are not as worthy of respect. The protector is seen as competent and capable and the person who needs to be looked after is seen as incompetent and incapable. This too is something which many women have begun to resist. These different understandings of independence are learnt in childhood as different pressures are exerted on males and females and it is going to take more than a little understanding of the other's point of view actually to change things. But a start has been made. Assertiveness training teaches us the standards and expectations of the opposite sex and helps us to begin to understand their different styles of communication. This does not mean that anyone of either sex should attempt to change his or her own style. A more realistic approach would be to learn how to interpret each other's messages and explain one's own in a way your partner can understand and accept. Once both men and women realize they have these different conversational styles, they will become more willing to accept differences without apportioning blame. They will accept that there is no 'right' way to speak, to have a conversation or to build a relationship. Nothing hurts more than being told you are wrong when in your heart you know you are doing something in the only way possible for you. Understanding these differences in ways of expression can take the bite out of them, and stop you feeling so 'put down' or patronzied. It may not prevent arguments but it may stop them from getting out of control and ultimately compromises may be easier to find. Understanding each other's conversational styles can form a bridge across the communication gap.

CHAPTER 10

Stress

Stress levels are usually higher amongst non-assertive people. They feel painfully self-conscious. So painful is it for some individuals that they avoid contact with others altogether. We must aim to exchange the self-consciousness for self-awareness. Self-awareness is a positive state of mind which enables people to take an objective view of themselves for the purpose of confirming that all is well. It allows the symptoms of stress to show themselves, to be recognized and dealt with. Self-awareness can be liberating and can give us a heady sense of freedom.

With the destruction of confidece, stress brings a lowered self-esteem and a fear of taking even the smallest risks. Society today seems to do little to help people who feel self-conscious, who blush, shake or stammer, but there is a lot they can do to help themselves. Dealing with stress is an important part of self-growth and the overcoming of all the fears associated with being non-assertive.

An overload of stress can hold you back in your career, your home-life and your personal life. Ultimately the whole quality of your daily existence suffers. How many times have you heard people remark that someone 'is not coping very well', 'is in a terrible state', or 'is a bundle of nerves'? The lives of people who suffer like this are certainly reduced in quality. Those who suffer from the effects of stress can become trapped in a circle of fear. This fear leads to reduced performance and reduced performance leads to even more fear. It is this reaction to fear that stops sufferers from enjoying life, from taking chances and from having fun. A reduction of your stress levels will help you gain the confidence to take some small steps towards assertiveness and improving your life in any area you decide.

Stressful reactions are produced as a response to all kinds of fear. The most common are fear of danger and fear of other people's reactions and opinions. And when your self-esteem or your pride are threatened you may become gripped by a terror just as real as the terror induced by fear of death.

When you feel frightened, the hormone adrenaline, various sugars and other stimulants are pumped through your system. Your eyes narrow and your muscles tense to prepare yourself for action. You begin to breathe more deeply and these deep breaths flood your system with another unwanted substance – an overdose of oxygen. These reflex reactions are instinctive and spontaneous responses to real OR perceived danger. The ensuing surge of chemicals clouds your thinking and renders even simple decision-making quite difficult.

Symptoms of stress can vary considerably from person to person. Shaking, sweating, erratic and racing heartbeat, nausea, vomiting, diarrhoea and pains in the stomach are all typical symptoms of stress. Add to this catalogue of unpleasant sensations headaches, tingling fingers, difficulties with eating and sleeping, depression, a dry mouth and bad temper and you begin to see the scale of the problem.

When you are stuck in traffic, when you are criticized or laughed at, your responses may be triggered. When you fear you might lose your job, your home or your loved one it is natural for you to react just as our ancestors did to the different kinds of fears that overwhelmed them. The spontaneous response to danger is kicked into action. In extreme cases a phobic reaction is triggered off by a simple stimulus.

The problem is that the hormones secreted into the system

in times of stress tend to get locked away. Instead of dealing with the danger by sprinting away or using this burst of energy to deal with the situation that set our hormones in action, we worry, we have nightmares and we panic. We take no positive action to burn up the chemicals. The result is that the stress stays within us for long periods of time, receiving regular 'toppings-up' whenever other feelings of doubt, apprehension or dread rise up inside us or when we find ourselves in situations we can't cope with. The vicious circle of reduced performance and increased stress levels continues. Persistently high stress levels can actually cause physical, mental and emotional damage.

If an engine isn't switched off from time to time it will overheat and may even explode. Our emotions experience a similar build-up too and unless we find ways to relieve it and find some kind of balance in our lives we will suffer a similar fate.

Most of us take our thoughts for granted. We don't realize how powerful they can be. Everything we are and everything we possess began as a thought. All kinds of creativity, every kind of education – even climbing Mount Everest – started as thought. Without thought we would not exist. So use it to your own advantage. Just as thinking negative thoughts will bring about negative results, if you 'accentuate the positive' you will achieve positive results. Yet, paradoxically, we do need some stress. Without it life would be meaningless, even dangerous. Stressful reactions can be vital when you need to run away from danger or need a surge of power to deal with a dangerous situation. I remember reading in a newspaper about a mum who needed superstrength to lift a car off her young son who had been run over. The release of the stress hormones gave her this extra strength and she saved her child's life. The extra power you find when these hormones come into action at times of huge and yet completely logical panic, can save your life and that of others. But if you get the same symptoms at inappropriate moments it can be very frightening. The secret is to find a balance between too little and too much stress at a pace that feels right for you.

A simple technique to release general stress and become more aware of yourself as an entity is to behave as animals do in the wild. Animals have no qualms about relaxing when they have exerted themselves. They simply lie down in a warm spot and recuperate. We can't always relax when we would like but we can recognize our stress levels and try, as far as possible, to indulge ourselves with a sweet moment of blissful relaxation when we get the chance. Your mind needs the rest just as much as your body.

There is a simple relaxation technique you can use at cocktail parties, trade fairs, or conferences or in any situation where you have to stand for long periods of time. Place your feet so they are the width of your hips apart and your weight is evenly balanced. Relax the muscles in your thighs and calves and lightly flex the knees. This will not only make you feel more confident but will make you look more confident too. Now breathe out and drop those hunched, tense shoulders, relax your neck and upper back muscles. Can you feel the wonderful release of tension?

Let your arms hang loose, relax, breathe deeply and release any other muscles you feel are tense - especially your stomach. This simple change in stance will hardly be noticed by anyone else around you but inside you will experience a sense of calm and you will notice a positive change in the way you feel.

If you are at work and things are getting on top of you try this way of relaxing to revitalize you. Sit comfortably with your feet squarely on the floor, close your eyes. Listen to your heartbeat, your rate of breathing and let your mind travel round your body and pick out the muscles which are tense. Breathe in through your nose; now slowly count to five and then breathe out again, counting to five. Repeat this exercise several times. You will soon begin to feel the tension ease.

This simple breathing and relaxation technique used for just five to ten minutes will quickly allow you to become more self-aware. You will grow calmer and the effects of stress will be reduced.

Even at home, most people are quite unused to sitting silently, reflecting on their feelings. It is more useful for them to flop on the couch and flick on the TV. Rarely does anyone take time to really relax, reflect and just be.

If you have a business or a house to run and a million and one thoughts queuing up to get into your mind you may feel guilty if you take this time for yourself. You will probably goad yourself on, reminding yourself that you should be doing this or that. Let these thoughts pass. After a few days you will have already started to feel better and you will begin to look forward to these uncluttered moments of your very own. Try taking a few minutes for yourself at the same point in each day so it becomes a habit which forms part of your daily routine and is less easy to forget.

We have already discussed how you can grow to like and accept yourself as you are. Now, during your private moments of solitude, don't compare yourself with others and dwell on your mistakes – start thinking of yourself as the valuable, unique individual that you are. Accept the fact that you are quite remarkable. There is only one 'you'. Celebrate your differences from others rather than considering them as faults in your personality. Once you stop comparing yourself with others you will become quite liberated and growth of your self-esteem will follow quite naturally.

Relaxation is a skill that is often left out during our formal education. Children are rarely allowed to simply do nothing. They are constantly being encouraged to learn, explore and succeed. If they aren't constantly on the go they are told they are lazy. They learn to fill their time with 'worthwhile' activities. Doing nothing in Western culture is condemned. We feel guilty if we are not always 'keeping on keeping on', aspiring, achieving.

When we recognize that our stress levels are high it is always a good idea to indulge ourselves with a sweet moment of blissful relaxation. You can take these moments whenever and wherever you can. On the bus, the train, at a concert, in the cinema or just sitting in your armchair. Your mind needs the rest just as much as your body. Whenever you get the opportunity to switch off, do so. You will be surprised at how much better you will begin to feel.

Don't worry. You are not alone in finding 'letting go' difficult to begin with. I get many letters from people asking 'How can I make myself relax?' The answer is – you cannot MAKE yourself do it. This implies hard work, surely the opposite of relaxation. It is true that the first few times, you do have to make a conscious effort until your way of relaxing becomes a 'programmed' reaction created by your repeated routines. Once you have learned how to let these calming waves flow over you, relaxation will become part of your life. All you have to do is to allow yourself this healing process. It is not a luxury.

The next step from relaxation is meditation – even more helpful in the battle against stress. If you don't know how to meditate here is an easy method. Sit comfortably and close your eyes. Focus your attention on your feet – ignore the rest of your body; it doesn't exist for the moment! After a while, move your centre of awareness to the top of your head. Wait a few seconds then move it to the centre of your chest. Then slowly move it around to other parts of your body until you feel comfortable about locating awareness of your physical self wherever you like. Drop your shoulders again. Then, gently allow yourself to become aware that you are one whole being. As you get used to this you will find your breathing will become slower and deeper. You can spend as long or as short a time as you like meditating in this way.

You are never too young or too old to learn to relax. You have the power to change your reactions to stress, to discard old habits and learn newer, healthier ones. You can change your physical bearing and your attitude and as a consequence you will become stronger. With a little effort you will begin to keep a cool head when you are in the hot seat and banish the unwanted effects of stress from your life for good.

YOGA

Yoga is an ancient relaxation technique which can help you reduce your stress levels and throw off the psychosomatic or 'nervous' illnesses that plague people today. It can help tighten the sagging muscles that give you that anxious or tired look. It can put new zest into your appetite, and with other relaxation techniques it can revitalize your whole system and bring back your sparkle. Yoga applies age-old secrets to everyday life at a tempo that works for us now as it did for the yogis of yesteryear. Just a few minutes' practical application each day can help put your whole body back in balance. It can revive feelings of lost youth and put new zest into everything you do.

Yoga is an art which has been developed and perfected over the centuries by the yogis or wise men of India. You can recognize elderly yogis in the market places of India by the joyful spring they have in their step, by their clear, undimmed eyes and by the straight, graceful posture of youth they carry even into very old age. Not only does yoga make you look and feel years younger, it can be remarkable in reducing levels of stress and increasing your feelings of wellbeing.

You will learn proper breathing to help with your relaxation. This will result in deeper, more beneficial sleep and a general sense of wellbeing. It helps you make the most of your inner resources. It promises a long, good and useful life, lived to the full and without fear. You can begin yoga at any age. Older people can take it up as well as the young and even children will benefit from it. It is true that the older person may not be able to attempt some of the advanced postures but a few minutes' practice of the simple basic movements can teach everyone the habit of relaxation. A limbering-up process for each pose is geared to the student's own pace so as not to overtax. Yoga can be integrated into anyone's life.

It is always wise to begin with a professional class. There are many classes run by local authorities. They are full of people of all ages and all walks of life. Yoga borrows from the animal world the secrets of alternative relaxation and tension, something that all living creatures, except man, seem to learn naturally. The schools of yoga are numerous but all have the same ultimate goal; to achieve profound mental and physical balance which makes it possible for the mind to soar. You can find out about classes from your local library or college of further education. You will find the shelves of shops and libraries full of books on the subject. These are valuable to help you work at home on your own once you have mastered the basic skills.

CHAPTER 11

Creative thinking

DREAM-TIME, BRAINSTORMING, AND 'YOUR COMMITTEE'

There are several ways to unblock your creativity and help you to make plans and deal with problems that may have been worrying you for a long time – things you have been going over and over in your mind and haven't been able to make a decision about. You may have a vague idea in your subconscious that the answer is there somewhere but you just can't seem to be able to put your finger on it. It is as if there is a huge brick wall between you and the answer to your problem.

DREAM-TIME

Everyone dreams. Some of us remember our dreams and some don't. Dreams have been used to help people solve their problems since biblical times. They have been defined as 'imagery during sleep'.

Discovering the meaning of dreams can be thought-provoking, and part of the process of the evolution of your assertiveness. They concentrate on the aspects of your personality that are being neglected during your daily life. They express underlying tension and they accompany inner growth and discovery.

Dream therapy has been distilled from the collective wisdom of Freud, Jung, Adler and the other psychotherapists we have discussed before.

Begin it by recording any dreams you can remember in your journal. Keep a notepad for night-time jottings by your bed which can be transferred to your journal later. Write as much as you can remember as soon as you wake, even in the middle of the night. Many is the time I have woken halfway through a dream. I've told myself, 'I will remember it in the morning' and lazily put off making an entry in my journal. By then the dream has slipped back into my unconscious and been lost for ever. However, if this does happen and the message conveyed by the dream is important it will come again, though possibly in a different guise. If you have difficulty recalling dreams, try to wake up more slowly and lie in a relaxed frame of mind for a minute or two. Try to remember the first thought that came to mind when you woke. This can either bring back the dream, or at least part of it, or it may throw some light on what the dream was trying to convey.

Remember that the writing down of your dreams too is for your eyes only, so don't miss any embarrassing bits out. There are times when everyone dreams about things which our 'civilized' mind would rather not have done but each part is vital and central to the picture that is being painted.

As you transfer your night-time record to your journal – ponder on it. Note down what feelings came up for you in your dream. Ask yourself whether it was happening today or in the past. Where were you? Were you at your present age? Was it during the day or was it night, morning or afternoon? What did it mean to you? By amplifying your dream in this way and looking closely at the order of the events you may begin to understand some of the links between events, sequences or images. Some people fear that thoughts about death, funerals or other morbid events are portents of doom and gloom but death in a dream is symbolic and may be interpreted at different levels. Death may be representing an ending, a changing, or a transformation. It may represent the death of a certain aspect of your life – the end of a job, a marriage or a relationship.

Dreams often produce frightening or powerful images which bear no resemblance to anything we understand in a logical or rational way. In instances like this we must work out the hidden image that is so important to us that it is trying to alert us. As you write out the content of your dream and the associated emotions, draw some pictures, try to bring it to life. If you cannot work out what it is telling you talk it over with some friends, who may be able to throw more light on it. Their opinions and interpretations will mean nothing to you if they are wrong but they may just strike a chord that makes it clear for you.

If you want to find out more specific information about your dreams you would be wise to enlist the help of a dream therapist, who understands the messages.

In typical dream analysis, an individual relates a dream and then lets his thoughts wander around why he thinks he had this dream. This is called free association. The point is to gain insight into underlying problems. Freud assumed that dreams were expressions of wish fulfilment. However, according to modern theory the meanings of dreams are interpreted through symbolism. The dream becomes a 'stand-in' or symbol for something else. The standard interpretations for some commonly occurring dream symbols are: towers, pencils, pistons and other objects of similar functional, physical or linguistic similarities are almost universally taken to be phallic symbols. Boxes, doorways and tunnels represent the vagina. However, it is misleading to generalize blindly about the symbolic elements of dreams on your own. If proper dream analysis is to be carried it should be done with a professional and it is best to avoid 'pop-psychology' books.

BRAINSTORMING

Brainstorming is another good way of looking at problems and finding new ways to deal with them. Turn to a fresh page in your journal. Write your problem at the top. Then put down every single idea that comes to mind when you try to find a solution to your problem. This doesn't just mean the sensible, practical, tangible, logical ideas that come from the adult part of your mind but the childish ones, the irrational and nonsensical ones too.

This is a good exercise to share with a friend. Instead of cramming all the ideas on a page in your journal you may like to spread a large piece of paper on the floor and take it in turns to add all the silliest and the cleverest ideas you can think of. Don't discuss them. Just write them down. It can be great fun and it can undo some of the emotional blocks that have been preventing you from solving your problem until now. Here is an example of a simple problem:

HOW CAN I KEEP MY OFFICE TIDIER?

- Spend the first half hour of the day tidying.
- Put everything in files so they are easier to find.
- Employ a cleaner to do the tidying for you.
- Get a filing cabinet.
- Throw away all the rubbish.
- Throw everything away!
- Get a fairy godmother to do it for you.
- Get a magic wand.
- Close the door and don't look at it.
- Invite your tidiest friend round for lunch.
- Put all the stuff in the garden shed.
- Get some boxes from the supermarket to put stuff in – label them.
- Get a clipboard for important bills etc.
- Have a different box for each month's bills.
- Paint one red for the urgent ones.
- Clear the decks every night.
- Get some coloured sticky labels so you can colour-code things.
- Get an accountant to sort it out.
- Get a friendly postman to help you sort it out.

• Forget all about it.

Once you get started you'll find you come up with some super ideas and you never know – you may even take some of the advice.

Get you friend to tell you one of her problems and do the same thing with her. Keep practising. Once you get the hang of it, have a go at a serious problem of your own. Start with a light-hearted one and go on to more complicated ones later.

Bear in mind that these are only ideas for you to practise with so you become used to this method of problem-solving. It is a good way of freeing your creativity and coming up with fresh ideas of your own.

'YOUR COMMITTEE'

This is a problem-solving technique often used in Gestalt Therapy. In this type of therapy a counsellor will ask you to arrange three chairs together. You will label each chair – your 'Adult', your 'Child', and your 'Parent'. You will write your problem on a card and put it on the floor in the space between the chairs. Then you sit on each chair in turn and rehearse to yourself the decision you are trying to make. The Child will say I want to do this. The Parent will say but you ought to do this. The Adult will give reasons for doing or not doing what the other two want. In this way you find a solution.

Alternatively you can have two chairs. Each holds a different viewpoint. A third chair, a little farther away, is labelled 'Director'. You sit in chair Number One and tell your imaginary partner what your idea is. Then you sit on chair Number Two and put up an argument. Give chair Number One all the reasons you can think of for carrying out your idea, including hunches and feelings. Then go back to chair Number One and examine it from the other side. Tell chair Number Two what is wrong with his ideas. Keep swapping all the ideas that come up. Be as logical and practical or as angry or as devious as you like. You may well discover the two warring parts to your personality which I have described before as the Id and the Ego, Positive and Negative, and so on.

When you have exhausted all the arguments sit on the empty Directors' chair and decide the best plan of action. You can discard all the irrelevant ideas, but think about the ones that will resolve the problem. It is surprising how a simple game like this will help unblock or release those blocked feelings.

When you are in the midst of an internal battle, when you can't make a decision, try tossing a coin. Heads you do this – tails you do that. Listen to your emotions. The feelings that are linked to the side of the coin that comes down uppermost will give you an important clue to what you really want. If the coin lands on the side you want, you will feel relief. You will find it easier to move in that direction. However if it lands on the side you really don't want, you will probably talk yourself into throwing it again – just to be sure. Once you have discovered your real feelings you will be more able to face what you must do to get what you want.

After reading this book I hope you will have discovered something more about assertiveness. Don't expect too much of yourself too quickly. Change happens slowly and there are always limitations. Assertiveness, like every other skill, has its off days. Old habits of the mind are difficult to shake off. But with a positive attitude and a healthy respect for yourself, your new assertive skills will begin to have a positive influence in your life, building up slowly and getting stronger with time and practise.

Being assertive is perfectly acceptable. We must stand up to those who do not respect our rights as human beings or they should be passed by – even long-standing relationships may be discarded. A new person is emerging who is not going to be walked over any more.

It is a perfectly natural phenomenon for the unpretentious nymph to metamorphose and emerge into the sunshine on a warm spring day as a fabulous dragonfly glowing with translucent colour. Change for human beings is as essential as it is for dragonflies. The only difference is that we can choose whether to change or not, whether to stay submerged in a dismal and limited world or whether to make some changes in order that we may start to spread our limpid wings and rise out of the depths. It's up to you.